GOOD

BETTER

BEST

Dining Out

GOOD BETTER BEST

Dining Out

A No-Nonsense Guide to America's Favorite Chain Restaurants

Josh Dinar

ALPHA

A member of Penguin Group (USA) Inc.

ALPHA BOOKS

Published by the Penguin Group

Penguin Group (USA) Inc., 375 Hudson Street, New York, New York
10014, USA • Penguin Group (Canada), 90 Eglinton Avenue East, Suite
700, Toronto, Ontario M4P 2Y3, Canada (a division of Pearson Penguin
Canada Inc.) • Penguin Books Ltd., 80 Strand, London WC2R 0RL, England • Penguin Ireland, 25 St. Stephen's Green, Dublin 2, Ireland (a division of Penguin Books Ltd.) • Penguin Group (Australia), 250 Camberwell
Road, Camberwell, Victoria 3124, Australia (a division of Pearson Australia
Group Pty. Ltd.) • Penguin Books India Pvt. Ltd., 11 Community Centre,
Panchsheel Park, New Delhi—110 017, India • Penguin Group (NZ), 67
Apollo Drive, Rosedale, North Shore, Auckland 1311, New Zealand (a division
of Pearson New Zealand Ltd.) • Penguin Books (South Africa) (Pty.) Ltd.,
24 Sturdee Avenue, Rosebank, Johannesburg 2196, South Africa • Penguin
Books Ltd., Registered Offices: 80 Strand, London WC2R 0RL, England

Copyright © 2012 by Josh Dinar

International Standard Book Number: 978-1-61564-143-7
Library of Congress Catalog Card Number: 2011936776

14   13   12   8   7   6   5   4   3   2   1

Interpretation of the printing code: The rightmost number of the first series of
numbers is the year of the book's printing; the rightmost number of the second
series of numbers is the number of the book's printing. For example, a printing
code of 12-1 shows that the first printing occurred in 2012.

Printed in the United States of America

Note: This publication contains the opinions and ideas of its author. It is
intended to provide helpful and informative material on the subject matter
covered. The author and publisher specifically disclaim any responsibility for
any liability, loss, or risk, personal or otherwise, which is incurred as a conse-
quence, directly or indirectly, of the use and application of any of the contents
of this book.

Trademarks: All terms mentioned in this book that are known to be or are
suspected of being trademarks or service marks have been appropriately capi-
talized. Alpha Books and Penguin Group (USA) Inc. cannot attest to the accu-
racy of this information. Use of a term in this book should not be regarded as
affecting the validity of any trademark or service mark.

Most Alpha books are available at special quantity discounts for bulk purchases
for sales promotions, premiums, fund-raising, or educational use. Special
books, or book excerpts, can also be created to fit specific needs.

For details, write: Special Markets, Alpha Books, 375 Hudson Street, New
York, NY 10014.

Contents

GOOD, BETTER, BEST DINING OUT

CONTENTS

Introduction

In Defense of the Chain Restaurant

It was 1996. I had been slogging through Africa and the Middle East for months with a small group of fellow travelers. Our backpacks were threadbare; we'd been "showering" with cold water scooped from buckets, washing a rotation of three T-shirts in whatever public sink or river we happened upon. We often had no idea how much money we had—it was impossible to keep conversion rates straight as we crossed border after border—but suffice it to say, it wasn't a lot.

Food was part of the experience, and in many ways we relished the chance to try each new and exotic national dish: ugali in Kenya, injera in Ethiopia, koshari in Egypt. We ate grilled goat meat (we think) from street vendors in Tanzania and nibbled at fish heads in a village in Uganda. But in 18 months of travel, one meal stood out above all others. We could hardly believe our eyes when we saw it, mere miles from the foot of the Pyramids of Giza, among the donkey-drawn carts and street merchants of bustling Cairo: that familiar red and green logo. Chili's.

That meal for us was a break from the unknown, and we slid into the familiarity—the pure "American-ness" of it—the way one might ease an aching body into a hot spa. Boneless Buffalo Wings, because really, who can be bothered with eating around the bone? Fried Cheese Sticks, the melted mozzarella stretching a full arm's length, from mouth to fingers. Bottomless chips and salsa … bottomless, I tell you! Tacos! Shrimp Fajitas! *Burgers!* The menu, replete with pictures of the food it described, was like a travel journal chronicling a home I missed terribly.

GOOD, BETTER, BEST DINING OUT

While uniformity is often part of the knock against chain restaurants, it's also their primary allure: the convenience and comfort of knowing exactly what you're going to get in a world that rarely affords such convenience and comfort.

Would I counsel eating nowhere but American chain restaurants while traveling away from home? Certainly not. I'm a firm believer that the character of a region—and the character of the people who make up the region—is reflected in the food you'll find exclusively in that place. But there's a global culture now, too, for better or worse, and there's something somehow reassuring in knowing that the Bloomin' Onion I get at the Outback Steakhouse in Colorado is the same one I can get in Chattanooga or San Diego or, for that matter, Guam.

And when you stop to think about it, that's pretty amazing in and of itself. Darden Restaurants, the group that owns iconic brands like Olive Garden and Red Lobster (among others), for example, employs more than 180,000 people and serves, as a company, more than 400 million meals a year. Of course, anything that big and corporate is a magnet for criticism, but this book isn't meant for the critics; it's meant instead to focus on us diners who make up those staggering statistics. Because when it comes right down to it, in one way or another, the restaurants explored in this book are reliably providing something a whole lot of people want.

The *something* however, varies from diner to diner, and from occasion to occasion.

And *that* is the point of *Good, Better, Best Dining Out*. I'm no longer a world-weary traveler. These days, I'm a week-weary professional, a husband, and a father of two. And while I'm still inclined to explore the great independent food scene wherever I am, I'm just as likely to need a convenient, affordable, well-balanced meal at a place where everyone I'm with can find something they like.

With that in mind, our team of editors set out to comb more than 4,000 menu items and amenities from 33 of America's most ubiquitous restaurants. As might be expected, we found many standouts worth highlighting, and those standouts are what you find described in the pages that follow. We've done our best to make this guide as comprehensive as possible, and we hope it helps you make the most of your next restaurant experiences. All that research has certainly helped us make the most of our waistlines!

Acknowledgments

First and foremost, I would like to thank Jeffrey Steen and Josh Tyson, editors extraordinaire. Without their hard work, diligent research, and carefree writing style, neither this book nor *DiningOut* magazine would exist. The credit for the vast majority of *Good, Better, Best Dining Out*'s content goes to them. I am, as always, proud of, humbled by, and indebted to their work.

The marketing teams at the restaurants profiled in these pages were, to varying degrees, helpful in navigating their restaurants' vast offerings. I would especially like to thank Alexis Aleshire, Jamie Winter, Travis Doster, Kristen Hauswer, Lauren Begley, and Kelly Thrasher for their assistance.

Lastly, I'd like to thank Marilyn Allen, the friendliest agent in the game, and Lori Cates Hand, our intrepid editor at Alpha Books. It was a great pleasure to work with both of you on this project.

Dining Out Basics

1

How to Use This Book

We designed *Good, Better, Best Dining Out* to help you navigate the most common aspects of the nation's most prolific restaurants. By design, this means there are many more restaurants *not* mentioned than those that are. Our goal was to create a guide you could use efficiently no matter where you live or travel. In so doing, we wanted to be sure the highlighted restaurants were among the most accessible across the widest audience.

All the restaurant brands we surveyed for this book are full-service, which eliminated fast-food chains like McDonald's and Burger King, quick-casual concepts like Panera Bread or Chipotle, and delivery/pickup stores like Domino's Pizza or Buffalo Wild Wings. We also narrowed the field by requiring a minimum of 75 domestic locations spread across all the regions of the country. These criteria winnowed most of the higher-priced chains such as Morton's Steakhouse, Capital Grille, and Maggiano's, leaving 33.

GOOD, BETTER, BEST DINING OUT

You'll note we've divided the book into broad categories—breakfast, appetizers, sandwiches, etc.—and that the chapters within each part compare our favorite standouts within those categories. You'll also see that not all dishes compared are necessarily apples to apples, or, in this case, Chicken Parmesan to Chicken Parmesan. Instead, we often emphasized creative takes on similar styles of cuisine. And while the lion's share of the book is dedicated to dissecting menus, most dining decisions also take into account aspects like service, ambiance, and amenity, all of which you'll find covered at the end of the book.

While the "good," "better," "best" sections are designed to help you decide where you want to eat, we also wanted to create a guide you could use when you're already at the table. For that reason, we created Chapter 2. In it, we highlight all the 33 restaurants surveyed, calling out the good, the better, and the best from within each of the individual menus.

Lastly, it's important to point out what we mean by "good," "better," and "best." All the dishes and features described in these pages are standouts in our estimation. Choosing which of the three took its place under the "best" designation was rarely an easy call. If it didn't make for a much clunkier title, we might have called this book *Very Good, Also Very Good, and Our Favorite by a Narrow Margin Dining Out.* In other words, you really can't go wrong, within the range of the establishments represented, by ordering any dish you'll read about in this guide.

A Word on Price

While price is often one of the primary factors in deciding where to eat, all the restaurants represented in these pages, when comparing like menu items, are in a very similar price range. We are unable to publish exact prices for specific menu items, both because those prices are subject to change from time to time and because prices vary (even within a single restaurant chain), depending on where in the country you are.

For these reasons, price comparison is not taken into consideration in a majority of the book.

Reviewing the Reviewers: Who We Are

My problem with restaurant reviews in nearly every case—whether the reviews are deeply researched, well-written magazine features or food-ignorant, grammatically abysmal web rants (or anything in between)—boils down to the fact that I don't know who's doing the reviewing. Just about the entire experience of dining out is both subjective and dependent on a combination of factors: food tastes, social preferences, occasion, mood, what's eaten in what combination, and so on. And while a good reviewer does his best to account for personal predilection—to base his review on the things that might be considered *objective*—there's just no way to remove personal taste from the act of *tasting things*.

A review, in the end, is really little more than an opinion. And while an opinion can be a great tool in decision-making, its usefulness is highly dependent on who's opining to whom. When my father tells me how much he loved a movie, for example, it's a pretty safe bet I'll hate it. In other words, if I'm going to take advice, I want to know whose advice it is I'm taking, so I can know how seriously I'm going to take it. All this is the long way around to introducing myself, and the others who worked on this book, so, at the very least, you know with whom you are agreeing or disagreeing as you read on.

GOOD, BETTER, BEST DINING OUT

As the co-founder and publisher of *DiningOut* magazine, I've been neck-deep in menus from around the country since the late 1990s. Together with long-time Senior Editors Jeff Steen and Josh Tyson (who are responsible for most of the research in this book), I've read and edited tens of thousands of food descriptions and grown fully fluent in "menu-ese," as we call it—a language with rhythms and rules all its own. We've seen the word *portobello* spelled more ways than Red Lobster does shrimp and borne witness to every possible potato permutation (creamy-Parmesan-wasabi-truffle-oil whipped fingerling mashed, anyone?). And like so many people, we love restaurants.

At *DiningOut*, as with *Good, Better, Best Dining Out*, we focus on highlighting that which we most appreciate within each regional dining scene, as opposed to focusing on the negative. Likewise, we're most interested in the things that differentiate one restaurant from another: quality and creativity, in that order. We prefer that things not be "dumbed down," but we'll take that over snobbery any day. We consider ourselves lucky to be in an industry that is, when it's done right, about inspiration and pleasure, about people gathering, and about providing a convenience or a respite or a celebration for those people. It's an industry that is, after all, about serving people—a highly personal and personality-driven experience. Dining at restaurants, no matter the restaurant, is a luxury, and we believe that luxuries, regardless how small, are crucial to the human spirit.

If you're not already familiar with our publication, you can flip through a recent edition, purchase gift certificates (many of which have exceptional bonus rewards attached to them), contact us directly, and find out how to bring *DiningOut* magazine to your city as a publisher at diningout.com. We would look forward to hearing your thoughts and dining experiences, and sharing them with others—whether they know who you are or not.

2

Restaurant Profiles

Numerous chain restaurants pepper the highways and byways of our great nation. That means numerous parent companies and many more outlets are selling steadfast favorites to throngs of hungry Americans.

To guide you along your culinary journey throughout the dozens of casual dining chains, in this chapter I give you a list of the 33 restaurants whose dishes populate these pages, along with a profile of each and a quick rundown of their top three offerings.

Applebee's

Dating back some 30 years, Applebee's was originally a Georgia native, though it has grown fairly steadily since its inception. Now boasting more than 1,900 restaurants across the world, Applebee's saw growth of about 100 restaurants per year between 1993 and 2005—its largest period of expansion. With a casual American comfort-food focus, the restaurant has tremendous appeal for diners of all ages and backgrounds.

Part of the chain's focus has been creating a family-friendly environment with food accessible to both kids and adults. The menu speaks for itself in this regard, spanning traditional burgers and ribs, as well as more worldly dishes like pasta and regional American creations from the South, the Midwest, and California.

As of 2007, Applebee's became part of the IHOP family—a buyout with a $1.9 billion price tag. It's a new future for Applebee's, and something to keep an eye on.

What's good, better, and best here?

- **Good:** Double-Glazed Baby Back Ribs
- **Better:** Hand-Battered Fish and Chips
- **Best:** Steakhouse Burger with A1 Sauce

Bennigan's

Where would American cuisine be without the import of Irish fare? Bennigan's is a tribute to the Irish tradition of taste in the New World, a place where chicken tenders meet Green Isle pot roast, and a pint is always a necessity with your meal.

The chain has been around since the mid-1970s and has expanded to global markets in its lifetime, reaching a peak around 2005. And while Irish pub fare is the concept, American dishes have proved just as popular, making this chain a true melting pot of flavor and culture.

In late 2010, Bennigan's began a revamp of the concept with dozens of new franchises opening across the country. Never fear, though—the same Irish-inspired cuisine will continue to be served at locations from east to west.

What's good, better, and best here?

- **Good:** Irish Dip
- **Better:** Drunken Pot Roast
- **Best:** Stacked Chicken and Shrimp

Big Boy

Surely you've seen the iconic chubby boy dressed up in checkered overalls—there's even a comic book series called *The Adventures of Big Boy*. Before the days of cartoon fame, however, Big Boy served as the inspiration for Bob Wian's new pantry/diner based in California. Now a successful franchise chain, Big Boy boasts more than 450 restaurants in the United States and Canada.

The food at Big Boy is simple but satisfying—no frills, just good-quality substance. The Big Boy Sandwich—one of the restaurant's first creations—was even the inspiration for McDonald's famed Big Mac. These days, Big Boy dishes up the same fare it always has, focusing on the important stuff: burgers, sandwiches, soups, salads, and breakfast.

What's good, better, and best here?

- **Good:** Chili Cheese Fries
- **Better:** Big Bleu Cheese Burger
- **Best:** Country Fried Steak

Bob Evans

Who would have thought sausage-making would lead to such a dynasty? Back in 1948, Bob Evans himself wouldn't have thought it possible, serving up his homemade sausage to guests at his 12-stool diner in Ohio. As his popularity grew, Evans decided to enter the restaurant business, and in 1962, he opened the first location on his farm.

These days, Bob Evans boasts 570 locations across the country, continuing to serve the same diner fare Evans himself served at the restaurant's inception.

Unknown to most, Mimi's Cafe—the American chain with French/New Orleans flair—is a wholly owned subsidiary of Bob Evans, broadening the reach of the Bob Evans company.

What's good, better, and best here?

- **Good:** French Toast
- **Better:** The Homestead Breakfast
- **Best:** Meatloaf and Gravy

Buca di Beppo

This favorite culinary son of Italian American heritage translates to something like "Joseph's basement," implying the casual, family nature of the restaurant. A young restaurant chain relative to its casual-dining cousins, Buca has been around since 1993 and now offers family-style southern Italian cuisine at 86 restaurants nationwide.

Originating in Minneapolis, Buca di Beppo has spread across the country with tremendous speed. In 2009, the chain premiered six new menu items for fans asking for more. Among them were Chicken Carbonara, Chianti-Braised Short Ribs, and spicy Shrimp Fra Diavolo.

What's good, better, and best here?

- **Good:** Veal Saltimbocca

- **Better:** Margherita Pizza
- **Best:** Linguine Frutti di Mare

California Pizza Kitchen

It started, as most great stories, with a great pizza. The first Pizza Kitchen opened in Beverly Hills in 1985, the brainchild of former federal prosecutors Rick Rosenfield and Larry Flax. True to its name, the California pizza trend—made popular by Wolfgang Puck—was taken up by California Pizza Kitchen (CPK), topping flavorful crusts with everything from barbecue sauce to Thai chicken.

Seven years after CPK came into being, it boasted 26 locations throughout southern California. These days, dozens dot the American landscape, dishing up everything from savory salads to a slew of inventive pizzas. The versatility of the menu, as well as the pizza itself, has made CPK a draw for hungry pie-lovers the country over.

What's good, better, and best here?

- **Good:** Pear and Gorgonzola Pizza
- **Better:** Jambalaya
- **Best:** Habanero Carnitas Pizza

Carino's Italian

Known by the loving public as Johnny Carino's, Carino's Italian (renamed circa 2009) proudly celebrated 170 restaurants across the United States at its peak just a few years ago. It's all about family and a unique twist on Italian food, which have always been mainstays in America.

A combination of individual-style dining and family dining, Carino's offers everything from panini to pizzas, pastas, and traditional Italian entrées. There's also an impressive selection of Italian-inspired cocktails, coffees, and desserts. Not to be behind the curve, Carino's also offers a selection of allergy- and diet-friendly dishes for diners.

What's good, better, and best here?

- **Good:** Spaghetti and Handmade Meatballs
- **Better:** Chicken Balsamico
- **Best:** Skilletini

The Cheesecake Factory

The pride and joy of Oscar and Evelyn Overton, The Cheesecake Factory had humble beginnings in 1972. It was in a 700-square-foot store that Evelyn began making her legendary cheesecake for the public while Oscar brought in new customers. Rapid success brought the Overtons a much-needed expansion in 1975, and, in 1978, the first Cheesecake Factory restaurant.

The concept at The Cheesecake Factory has always been "generous portions with unlimited, inventive menu selections all made fresh with quality ingredients and served in a warm and casually comfortable setting." An obvious success, the restaurant now boasts about 150 locations and more varieties of cheesecake than you can shake a stick at.

What's good, better, and best here?

- **Good:** Crusted Chicken Romano
- **Better:** Godiva Chocolate Cheesecake
- **Best:** Pumpkin Pecan Cheesecake

Whole Lotta Cheesecake

Boasting more than 50 legendary cheesecakes and desserts, how can you talk about The Cheesecake Factory and not mention cheesecake? Unfortunately, however, some cheesecakes are seasonal, including the Pumpkin Pecan Cheesecake. It's served only between October and the holidays, so put a trip to The Factory on your fall calendar.

Chili's

Dallas served as home to this Southwestern/American grill back in 1975—a propitious year for restaurant openings, it seems. And the mantra has been the same for the last 30-some years: create a family-friendly environment, unbeatable hospitality, and of course, great food.

Truth be told, the original Chili's was a humble post office–turned–burger joint, purportedly started by a chili cook-off winner who got an idea for a restaurant. Lucky for him, the idea took off, and Chili's has been dishing up American fare in a comfortable (albeit unique) setting since its inception.

What's good, better, and best here?

- **Good:** Hatch Chile Cheeseburger
- **Better:** Crispy Honey Chipotle Chicken Crispers
- **Best:** Baby Back Ribs

Margarita, Please!

In 1982, Chili's was serving 25¢ margaritas. That's 4 for $1. Boggles the mind.

Cracker Barrel

Designed much like a country store-cum-farm, this one-time small-town establishment has found appeal in cities all across the United States. Dan Evins, the company's founder, was inspired to open Cracker Barrel to meet the needs of folks traveling on America's highways. He wanted to create a place where mealtime was more than just a chance to get something to eat—it was a chance for families and friends to catch up.

The first Cracker Barrel opened in Lebanon, Tennessee, in 1969. These days, Cracker Barrel has seen many a highway traveler in its more than 600 locations in 42 states. And whether you're looking for a meal or a chance to browse through the knick-knacks in the country store, you'll quickly see why Cracker Barrel has become such a staple in America.

What's good, better, and best here?

- **Good:** Grandpa's Country Fried Breakfast
- **Better:** Homemade Chicken n' Dumplins
- **Best:** Smoked Country Sausage n' Biscuits

Denny's

Dubbed "America's diner," Denny's has had a nationwide presence for decades. Conceived in 1953—the golden age of diners—Denny's first began as a doughnut shop. By 1953, however, the popularity was rising and founder Harold Butler decided it was time to add some savory dishes to the menu. By 1959, there were 20 restaurants in the successful chain—and growing.

Part of what the public associates with Denny's is its famous Grand Slam Breakfast. Created in 1977, it was originally a nod to baseball great Hank Aaron. The fame of breakfast—and all the restaurant's diner fare—grew exponentially. By 2009, Denny's boasted more than 1,500 restaurants across the United States, all sporting the welcoming character of Butler's original restaurant.

What's good, better, and best here?

- **Good:** All-American Slam
- **Better:** Ultimate Skillet
- **Best:** Sweet and Tangy BBQ Chicken

Hard Rock Cafe

Hard Rock is more than just a restaurant—it's a cultural icon. If you've ever traveled overseas, your bucket list has probably included a visit to Hard Rock Cafes in any number of the world's capital cities. Why? Because it stands for something—not only for American culture, but for philanthropy and hospitality.

A fan favorite since 1971 when it was first opened in London, Hard Rock has focused on three things: rock and roll, hospitality, and Americana. And while menus do change from cafe to cafe, the concept remains the same: burgers, classic smokehouse fare, salads, and sandwiches. Keep it simple; keep it American; keep it rock and roll.

What's good, better, and best here?

- **Good:** Hickory-Smoked Chicken Wings
- **Better:** Hickory-Smoked Bar-B-Que Chicken
- **Best:** S.O.B. Burger

Hooters

I'll bet you didn't know the real design inspiration for Hooters was the beach. It's true—oh, and sexy women. Old-time jukeboxes and big-screen TVs dot each restaurant, but the focus is really the food. And the women. In the words of Hooters, "Hooters Girls have the same right to use their natural female sex appeal to earn a living as do super models Cindy Crawford and Naomi Campbell." Enough said.

Back to the food, though. The menu offers decidedly American sports-bar fare, from wings to burgers. There are salads, too, and your traditional sandwiches, but as the typical demographic here is male, ages 25 to 54, there's also a distinct focus on large portions, big cup size, and well, you get the idea.

What's good, better, and best here?

- **Good:** Ribs Platter
- **Better:** Buffalo Chicken Sandwich
- **Best:** Bleu Cheese Burger

> **Hooters Air**
> Did you know there was a Hooters Air airline that operated between 2003 and 2006? Rumor was Hooters Hotels were in talks, too. Too bad that never happened.

IHOP

In 1958, one of America's most well-known breakfast staples opened to a hungry public in a Los Angeles suburb. Little did founders Al and Jerry Lapin know that their International House of Pancakes (IHOP) would, in fact, gain international notoriety.

One of IHOP's more recent offerings reinvigorated the country's love of fair fare—that is, the beloved funnel cake. And in 2008, IHOP celebrated 50 years of serving up griddle cakes, waffles, and palate-pleasing breakfast dishes.

These days, IHOP boasts 1,522 locations across the U.S. of A. Expanding every day, it's no wonder the Lapins' concept has tickled the hearts and tummies of Americans everywhere. After all, who doesn't like breakfast?

What's good, better, and best here?

- **Good:** CINN-A-STACK Pancakes
- **Better:** Smokehouse Combo
- **Best:** Chicken Florentine Crépes

Johnny Rockets

When you think Johnny Rockets, you think *American Graffiti*—the golden age of sock hops and soda shops. But the charm is in its universality—it's all about feel-good America at Johnny Rockets, and while a lot of that comes to us courtesy of the 1950s and '60s, it embraces all generations.

In its 20-some-year tenure (opening in 1986), Johnny Rockets has been serving up simple but classic burgers, sandwiches, shakes, and malts. Authentic Americana décor gives each restaurant an even more classic feel, recalling memories of the past while living in a very dynamic present.

What's good, better, and best here?

- **Good:** Route 66 Burger
- **Better:** Smoke House Double Burger
- **Best:** Chili Dog

> **Shake It Up**
> When you're ordering at Johnny Rockets, do consider adding an original Vanilla Shake to your order.

Logan's Roadhouse

Founded in Kentucky, Logan's has spread to a meaty 200+ locations in 23 states. This is really what a steakhouse is all about: mesquite-grilled steaks, yeasty rolls, and more than 50 entrées. With that much selection, it's hard not to find something that makes you hungry.

The ambience, meanwhile, calls on flavors of steakhouses past while remaining in tune with contemporary life. It's kickin', it's comfortable, and it's hospitable. In Logan's own words, this is one steakhouse that has become "a real American tradition."

What's good, better, and best here?

- **Good:** MeatHeads
- **Better:** Roadhouse Steak Melt
- **Best:** Onion Brewski Sirloin

> **Growin' Fast**
> Logan's Roadhouse was first opened in 1991, which means it opened an average of 10 new restaurants a year since its inception.

LongHorn Steakhouse

LongHorn is all about passion—passion for steaks, passion for service, passion for all things dining. So says their tag line: "The West of loyalty, hospitality, and of course, real good food."

When it comes to the food, the key for LongHorn is never to serve anything frozen—from steaks and chicken to salmon and ribs. More than 350 locations prove that to be true, garnering a loyal following that treats LongHorn like a second home. The idea here is to relax, unwind, and let yourself be taken care of.

Inspired by the American West, LongHorn maintains a tradition of decorating each restaurant with Western memorabilia recalling some of the country's greatest moments in history.

What's good, better, and best here?

- **Good:** Steakhouse Dinner for Two (limited time offer)
- **Better:** Flo's Filet
- **Best:** Cowboy Pork Chops

Mimi's Cafe

World War II brought us much—including the end to a severe depression, a renewed patriotism, the end of isolationism … and a re-introduction to Continental cuisine.

Mimi's, one bold and lasting tribute to those glory days, was the brainchild of WWII Airman Arthur J. Simms. Stationed in France during the war, Simms fell in love with the flavors and beauty of France. This love incubated following the end of conflict, and in 1978, it blossomed into what we now know as Mimi's Cafe—a neighborhood bistro recalling those in mid-century France.

GOOD, BETTER, BEST DINING OUT

What's good, better, and best here?

- **Good:** Crab Fritters
- **Better:** Turkey Pesto Ciabatta
- **Best:** Salmon Provence Salad

Who Was Mimi?

The name Mimi's Cafe is derived from the name of a certain mademoiselle Airman Simms met while stationed abroad. Word has it, he was quite taken with her.

O'Charley's

Casual family dining is the name of the game at O'Charley's—an experience that's both accessible and adventurous. One of the restaurant's signatures is their hot-out-of-the-oven rolls. An O'Charley's welcoming treat, the rolls have become a draw for diners in 18 states.

One of O'Charley's charms, setting it aside from fellow restaurants, is its delicious brunch. Linger or come in late—brunch here is no rush. The idea is all about relaxing and enjoying your meal, so sip, munch, and savor. A staple of the Southeast and Midwest, O'Charley's is without a doubt an American tradition.

What's good, better, and best here?

- **Good:** O'Charley's Baby Back Ribs
- **Better:** Prime Rib Pasta
- **Best:** Chicken Bacon Bleu Sandwich

Olive Garden

Genuine Italian, that's what the Garden is about. With a family of more than 750 locations, their cry for greatness rings loud and clear in every restaurant: "*Hospitaliano!*"

As the team at Olive Garden would say, Italy is the inspiration for everything the restaurant is about—from the pictures on the wall to the pasta in your bowl. One of the Garden's claims to fame is the Olive Garden Culinary Institute of Tuscany (no, it's not something they just made up). Every year, employees spend time at the Institute to learn more about the food, the culture, and the environment. When they come back, Italy is in their blood.

What's good, better, and best here?

- **Good:** Roasted Mushroom Parmesan
- **Better:** Stuffed Mushrooms
- **Best:** Steak Gorgonzola Alfredo

"Bottomless" Defined

At Olive Garden, "bottomless" means you get endless breadsticks and salad forever and ever until you can literally hold no more. To clarify, "forever" in this equation means for the duration of your visit, but if you want to relive the salad experience at home, they have dressings for sale.

Outback Steakhouse

Outback—it's Australian for "steak." True story. The restaurant company, which now has its headquarters in Miami, was originally looking at creating delicious food, generous portions, and moderate prices—inspired by the

Australian Outback. More than just a place to come for dinner, Outback prides itself on being adventurous and fun—but not so adventurous you forget why you came there to eat.

Found in 1988, Outback is still a young buck in the restaurant world but has proved to be very successful, now tallying 1,200 locations across the world. Because, I mean, who doesn't love a great steak with a pint of Fosters?

What's good, better, and best here?

- **Good:** Alice Springs Chicken
- **Better:** Bloomin' Onion
- **Best:** Victoria's Filet

P.F. Chang's

It's time to pop the sake corks—P.F. Chang's is enjoying 18 years of business bliss, dished up in chain restaurant form. Unique and beautiful in its own right, P.F. Chang's has many dimensions to its personality—made up of both food and ambience.

The art that marks each restaurant is inspired by a much older time—twelfth-century China, as a matter of fact. No doubt you've seen the imposing horse statues (each 11 feet high) that greet every diner, and perhaps you've glanced at the expansive murals in the dining rooms. They all conjure history and tradition, both of culinary ages long since, and a culture that continues to inspire societies the world over.

The food at P.F. Chang's is no afterthought. Truly authentic and filled with flavors from across China, it's no wonder there are 200 locations across the world.

What's good, better, and best here?

- **Good:** Crab Wontons
- **Better:** Mandarin Chicken
- **Best:** Chang's Chicken Lettuce Wraps

Perkins

Half a century after its humble beginnings as an Ohio pancake house, Perkins sticks to its guns as a family restaurant offering the best in service, quality, and value. Operating in 34 states and 5 Canadian provinces, each outpost offers a full menu of more than 90 breakfast, lunch, and dinner delights.

Signature hits include omelets, "secret recipe" buttermilk pancakes, Mammoth Muffins, salads and melts, and breakfast any time of day. But the real attraction here is a totally unique atmosphere that combines the bright and airy with the cozy and comfy in ways that defy mere words. Perkins is the place for affordable comfort.

What's good, better, and best here?

- **Good:** Country Cookin' Benedict
- **Better:** Chicken Pot Pie
- **Best:** Perky Bear Pancakes

Red Lobster

When you're the Red Lobster, the ocean just gives it up. Why? Because Red Lobster is the big red daddy of seafood restaurants. What lobster tail wouldn't want to be served up on a platter here? TLC has always been part of the game.

Company founder Bill Darden was just 19 when he opened his first restaurant, The Green Frog—putting the focus on quality and service since day 1. Over the years, Red Lobster has given patrons their first tastes of calamari, snow crab, and Key lime pie—and has given the world the fabulous invention of popcorn shrimp. Now numbering more than 680 North American locations, Red Lobster is bigger than ever but keeps its mistress in fine linen, making strides toward using the most sustainable business practices available.

What's good, better, and best here?

- **Good:** Ultimate Feast
- **Better:** Rock Lobster Tail
- **Best:** Mozzarella Cheese Sticks

Red Robin

As much a philosophy on service as a restaurant, Red Robin got its start in the Pacific Northwest (Seattle, to be exact) more than 40 years ago (1969, to be exact), adhering to the same principles that make it such a stalwart favorite throughout North America. Those principles: honor, integrity, the eternal pursuit of knowledge, and fun!

It doesn't take long for the Red Robin way to show its colors. Step inside, and you're immediately caught up in the vibrant atmosphere. Part of the flagship fun is the Smiling Burgers (which equal smiling guests) and giving guests "moments" rather than just "minutes." High-minded but sure-footed—that Red Robin.

What's good, better, and best here?

- **Good:** Towering Onion Rings
- **Better:** Whiskey River BBQ Chicken Wrap
- **Best:** The Banzai Burger

Romano's Macaroni Grill

The simplicity of authentic Italian food is its own comfort—but sometimes it's hard to find outside the boot. Enter Romano's Macaroni Grill—a paean to innovative Italian cooking and inspiring wines. For more than 20 years, the Grill has been bringing regional Italian dishes to our tables, furthering America's love of Italian cuisine.

Among the more notable facts about Romano's Macaroni Grill is their commitment to sourcing ingredients from Italy. Their cold-pressed olive oil, for example, comes from Italy, along with bronze-cut pasta, the tomatoes for the Pomodorino Sauce, limoncello, and an 8-year aged balsamic vinegar.

The whole point? Make each meal feel like something special—a celebration, a gathering of friends and family, or an intimate night out. The response has been overwhelming, firing the opening of more than 200 locations across the country.

What's good, better, and best here?

- **Good:** Shrimp, Cannellini Bean, and Avocado Crostini
- **Better:** Wild Mushroom and Goat Cheese Flatbread
- **Best:** Carbonara

Ruby Tuesday

"Good-bye, Ruby Tuesday," goes the Rolling Stones' song that inspired this longtime fave, but "Hello, Ruby Tuesday" go its many devotees. Freshness, quality, and gracious hospitality are the core tenets of operations here, and they come to life as the warm and engaging staff delivers handcrafted burgers that are the stuff of legend— or point the way to the equally beloved Fresh Garden Bar.

Sandy Beall started Ruby Tuesday back in 1972, opening the original location near the University of Tennessee—hoping to bring the area someplace casual and comfortable that looked great. His gamble paid off, as Ruby Tuesday now boasts 900 locations worldwide.

What's good, better, and best here?

- **Good:** Lobster Carbonara
- **Better:** Memphis Dry Rub Baby-Back Ribs
- **Best:** Freshly Made Soup and Salad

Shoney's

For more than six decades, Shoney's has been serving Americans casual comfort food, with humble origins as a drive-in in Charleston, West Virginia, keeping its heart in the right place. Visit a Shoney's in its home state or neighboring Kentucky on a Sunday evening, and it's not uncommon to see a family, still dressed for church, enjoying a traditional meal together.

A big favorite here is the breakfast buffet, a bit of an anomaly in chain-resto land. Those living within the hospitality belt—an informal stretch of states where the Shoney Bear roams, running down the eastern seaboard from Maryland, lifting up into the Midwest, and swooping

through Texas and into New Mexico—line up good and
early for this weekend morning mainstay.

What's good, better, and best here?

- **Good:** Hand-Breaded Chicken Strips
- **Better:** Pile O' Shrimp
- **Best:** Slim Jim

Texas Roadhouse

Texas Roadhouse got its start in the great state of Indiana.
The year was 1993, and Kent Taylor was itching to create
a truly family-friendly steakhouse. Part of that approach
has always included making the employees feel as though
they are part of a family—the thinking being that happy
employees equals happy customers. The success of this
idea is perfectly illustrated by the T-shirts worn by staff
that read "I ❤ My Job!"

As for the food, expect lots of handcrafted sides and stellar
meat preparations, including hand-cut steaks. "We've
got the great meal part down," TexasRoadhouse.com
proclaims. "In fact, we like to consider our food more than
great. We think it's Legendary." Indeed, a legend as big as
old Texas herself.

What's good, better, and best here?

- **Good:** Cactus Blossom/Fried Pickles
- **Better:** Road Kill
- **Best:** Bone-In Rib-Eye

T.G.I. Friday's

Everyone's favorite anagram became everyone's favorite restaurant way back in 1965, if you can believe it. And T.G.I. Friday's is quick to claim OG status (that's Original Gangster, y'all) on creating "what is now referred to as the casual dining industry." This fun factory was born when New Yorker Alan Stillman bought a bar on 1st Avenue and 63rd Street with the primary goal of meeting stewardesses. But fate had other ideas.

Originally a swinging singles bar, T.G.I. Friday's has evolved into a family-friendly spot to grab a meal with the kids or drinks with friends and/or possible lovers. What's remained the same is Stillman's love of whimsy, with a lively and unmistakably upbeat vibe. And while we're doling out credit, T.G.I. Friday's also invented the world-famous Loaded Potato Skins.

What's good, better, and best here?

- **Good:** Loaded Potato Skins
- **Better:** New York Cheddar and Bacon Burger
- **Best:** Ultimate Mudslide

ULTIMATE! MUDSLIDE!!
This exciting cocktail is practically a meal in itself—Kahlúa, vodka, Bailey's, and ice cream. If only there were a way to live off these things (without losing your job, that is).

Tony Roma's

Tony Roma's once gave itself billing as "A place for ribs," but it's equally beloved for their signature onion ring loaf. So it's no surprise that while the ribs are still central (and gooey … and tangy … and delicious) the menu has branched out to include something for just about everyone—soups, salads, seafood, sandwiches—flatbreads even. Still, Tony Roma's remains the world's largest restaurant chain specializing in ribs, with almost 200 locations scattered worldwide.

The original Tony Roma's opened in North Miami in 1972. Baby back ribs quickly rose to prominence, and people began traveling miles to sample this signature fave. In January 1976, Clint Murchison Jr., owner of the Dallas Cowboys, was in Miami for the Super Bowl and made the journey himself. Not long after licking his fingers clean, he offered to purchase U.S. franchise rights and begin expansion. The rest is tender, fall-off-the-bone history.

What's good, better, and best here?

- **Good:** The Original Baby Back Ribs
- **Better:** Onion Loaf
- **Best:** Beef Short Rib

Village Inn

Village Inn has been a comfort-food contender since 1958, thanks in no small part to friendly service and a clean family-friendly environment. Made-from-scratch buttermilk pancakes, eggs cooked to style, and a pot of hot coffee on your table are the tried-and-true trademarks here.

Also hugely popular are wares of the Village Inn Skillet Experts—that's breakfast skillets, in case you missed it.

Village Inn corporate and franchise restaurants total more than 200 in the Rocky Mountains, the Midwest, Arizona, and Florida. A recent design revamp has given the restaurant a current retro look (not an oxymoron, really), but the breakfast, lunch, and dinner delights remain as steady and delicious as ever.

What's good, better, and best here?

- **Good:** Ultimate Breakfast
- **Better:** Crépes Lorraine
- **Best:** Double Bacon Double Cheese Skillet

Waffle House

Founded by Joe Rogers Sr. and Tom Forkner, who met when the latter sold a house to the former, the first Waffle House opened on Labor Day 1955 in Avondale Estates, a suburb of Atlanta. The friendliest service in town was there at the get-go, customer loyalty and demand grew in kind, and by 1961, five Waffle House restaurants were in operation.

Before long, the happy yellow sign became a beacon along interstate highways and city streets across the Southeast. In-house traditions, like a jukebox in every restaurant and 24/7 access to delicious morning fare, are almost family traditions for plenty of customers (and have inspired urban legends such as "There are no locks on the doors"), making Waffle House something of a national icon.

What's good, better, and best here?

- **Good:** Papa Joe's Pork Chops
- **Better:** Texas Biscuits and Gravy
- **Best:** Sweet Cream Double Waffle

PART

2

Breakfasts

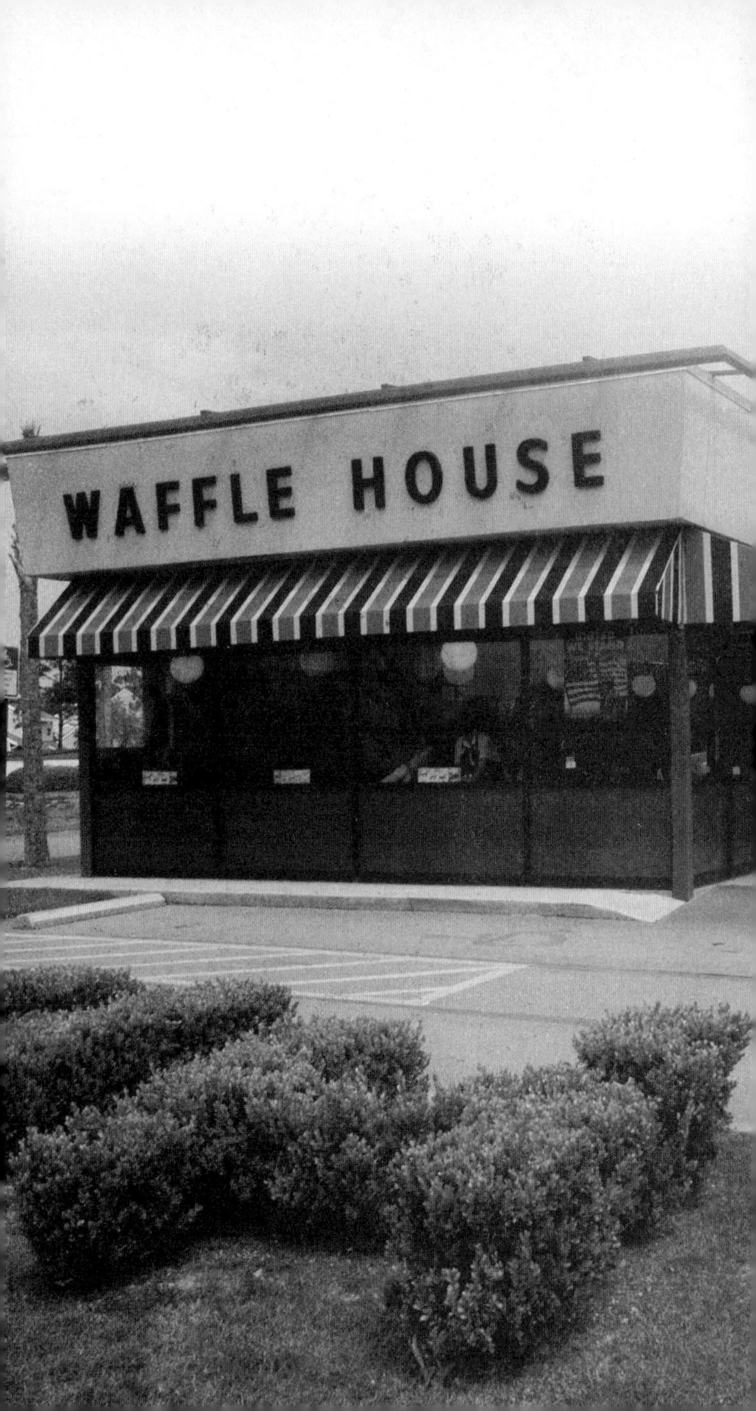
WAFFLE HOUSE

3

Egg Dishes

Perhaps no other meal of the day demands as much consistency and precision as breakfast. Everyone likes his or her breakfast just so, and it's a minefield for any chef, but the line cooks at our beloved chain restaurants have it down past science. And of course, the science of breakfast almost always starts with eggs.

Eggs, eggs, eggs. Eggy, weggy, leggy eggs. Slow-cooked eggs, scrambled eggs, poached and fried and folded eggs. You can have a lot of fun with eggs, but eggs are also serious business. Nature worked her buns off creating a perfect food—so adaptable, so structurally secure, so full of good nutrition—and the dishes chronicled on the pages that follow pay fine homage to her brilliance.

BENEDICTS

GOOD

BETTER

Perkins' Florentine Benedict

This one's for the calorie counters. Clocking in at just 420, this petite beauty is made with Egg Beaters, Canadian bacon, spinach, sliced tomatoes, and Swiss cheese. Demure though she may be, the Florentine still brings the flavor. Rather than saddle this healthy choice with potatoes, a side of fresh fruit makes this a wise way to start the day.

Perkins' N'awlins Benedict

Marinated shrimp? Check. Cajun grilled chicken? Check. Smoked sausage? Yes, that, too—and diced tomatoes and two basted eggs on a toasted English muffin. But it's probably the chipotle hollandaise sauce that gets mouths watering every time. That and the choice of hash browns, breakfast potatoes, or the Mammoth Muffin (more on this guy in Chapter 5).

BEST

Village Inn's Farmer's Market Potato Pancake Benedict Scrambler

This Benedict is one of three newfangled takes on the breakfast stalwart—each boasting a hot potato pancake in place of an English muffin and eggs scrambled rather than poached or basted. Here, our newcomers meet sautéed artichokes, mushrooms, spinach, tomatoes, and melted Swiss before being enveloped by tomato-basil hollandaise sauce.

The First Eggs Benedict

Eggs Benedict is a dish with several origin stories, but this one seems most poetic: Retired Wall Street broker Lemuel Benedict staggered into the Waldorf Hotel in 1894 looking for a cure for his hangover. He ordered "buttered toast, poached eggs, crisp bacon, and a hooker [or good slug] of hollandaise." The hotel's famous maître d', Oscar Tschirky, was impressed to the point of putting it on the breakfast and lunch menus—swapping ham and a toasted English muffin for the bacon and toast. Now that's teamwork.

GOOD

BETTER

Perkins' Granny's Country Omelet

The diced ham, onions, American cheese, celery, and green bell peppers say "Welcome to Granny's kitchen." The cheese sauce poured over the top says "Welcome to flavor country." Perkins' signature hash browns folded inside and lingering next to this geometrically pleasing and fluffy sight just say "Welcome," making this one hard to pass up.

Waffle House's Cheesesteak Omelet

What's better than a cheesesteak sandwich? If you answered "Nothing," good for you, because there is literally nothing greater, but points to our favorite house of waffles for bringing the allure of nature's finest sandwich into the realm of the A.M. Yes, steak, sautéed onions, American cheese—it's all here in this marvelous, marvelous omelet.

BEST

Village Inn's Ultimate Bacon and Cheese Omelet

There's no need to mess with simple, pure perfection, and Village Inn knows it. For evidence, examine this omelet: diced, hickory-smoked bacon, a gang of four cheeses inside (cheddar, Jack, American, and cream), and a fifth melted over the top (mozzarella). This is everything an omelet should be.

GOOD

BETTER

Village Inn's Rio Grande

A choice of grilled chicken or pork carnitas sets the stage for an awesome skillet wherein red bell peppers, onions, fire-roasted pork, and green chili create heat and tang to complement the creamy blankets of pepper Jack, Jack, and cheddar cheeses—all on a bed of country potatoes, of course. That this creation comes standard with a side of buttermilk pancakes only ups the delicious ante.

Denny's Bananas Foster French Toast Skillet

Points for thinking outside the skillet, Denny's. This cast-iron creation eschews the standard eggs and potatoes foundation for something different: two slices of thick French toast bathed in caramel sauce and dappled with sliced bananas. Eggs and choice of bacon or sausage come on the side, as not to disrupt this artistic presentation.

BEST

Bob Evans' Sunshine Skillet

Take an omelet, open it up, fill it with Bob Evans' trademark sausage and home fries, drown that in country gravy and melted cheddar, put it in a bowl (in effect making the eggs the skillet—brilliant), and make breakfast dreams a reality. Why can't everything in life be this simple?

4

From the Griddle

Breakfast all goes back to that keystone consistency we've been talking about. The crucible of the chain restaurant is the pancake at the Hoboken, New Jersey, outpost having the exact same sponginess and richness as the cake that comes off of their griddle in Fresno, California. One more time for the cheap seats: consistency, consistency, consistency—this is the chain restaurant version of the real estate mantra: location, location, location.

We Westerners tend to take our nonstick, tempered griddles for granted. After all, only a few hundred years ago a griddle was a brick or screaming hot stone in a fire. These days, nearly every home in the land has something hot, flat (or pocketed, where waffles are concerned), and relatively high tech for turning batter into beauty. Our friends at the favorite chains have them even bigger— perfect for cranking out (*consistent!*) legions of perfect pancakes, waffles, and dipped toast.

FRENCH TOAST

GOOD

BETTER

Perkins' Ooh-La-La French Toast

Go ahead and order these loud and proud: "The Ooh-La-La French Toast, if you please!" You won't be sorry, for these five demure slices of French bread are hand-dipped in an inspired batter of eggs, vanilla, and cinnamon and then griddled just right. Perkins brand syrup under a dollop of whipped butter paints a pretty picture indeed—*ooh-la-la!*

Denny's French Toast Slam

The Denny's Slam is a tough dunk to top. Here you'll find two austere slabs of succulent French toast alongside two eggs, two strips of bacon, and two sausage links. It's the total package that makes the sale, for a bite of this crisp griddle wonder forked with a bit of bacon or sausage and drawn through syrup is nothing short of breakfast nirvana.

FRENCH TOAST

Saving Lost Bread

In France, French toast is called *pain perdu,* or "lost bread." This is because dredging hunks of a day-old baguette in a milk and egg mixture served as a way of saving bread that would otherwise be lost. Thus, you are a hero when you eat French toast.

BREAKFASTS

IHOP's Stuffed French Toast Combo

French toast and indulgence are perfect bedfellows, so it makes sense that these are the top of the crop. Cinnamon raisin French toast with a sweet cream filling, dressed with those cool strawberries, warm blueberries, or a cinnamon apple compote and whipped topping. Served with two eggs, hash browns, two bacon strips or two pork sausage links.

BEST

49

GOOD

Perkins' The Buttermilk Five

Five buttermilk pancakes made from a secret batter recipe. Five buttermilk pancakes made from a secret batter recipe. Five buttermilk pancakes made from a secret batter recipe.

BETTER

Denny's Grand Slam

These days, you build your own Grand Slam at Denny's, and although you have the choice of any four items off of a long list of breakfast favorites—including buttermilk biscuits, grits, hash browns, turkey bacon, and oatmeal—it never fills one, if not two of those slots with Denny's spongy, velvety buttermilk pancakes. A double order looks great on the plate next to a double order of bacon.

BEST

IHOP's CINN-A-STACK Pancakes

Are these a bit over-the-top? You bet, but sometimes the rules of healthy eating are meant to be broken. Four buttermilk pancakes layered with cinnamon roll filling, drizzled with cream cheese, and topped with whipped cream can only mean one thing. Well, it could mean a few things, but for the sake of argument, it means sticky, sugary deliciousness.

A Pancake by Any Name …

Pancakes are so old and important a food, nearly every region on the planet has a variation. France has crêpes, Germany has Pfannkuchen, the West Indies has johnnycakes, India has pooda, Japan has okonomiyaki, and Antarctica has delicious thin sheets of ice.

51

WAFFLES

GOOD

BETTER

IHOP's Belgian Waffle

This is a Belgian waffle to a T—thick with a crunchy exterior that breaks, giving way to a moist and slightly fluffy interior. Shaped by the griddle into four triangular sections, this lovely specimen begs dissection and can be dressed up in myriad ways. Warm blueberries, cinnamon-apple compote, or cool strawberries, each brings its own complement to this wonder of batter and heat.

Perkins' Belgian Waffle

It was almost too close to call between the Belgians at IHOP and Perkins, but what cinched it in the end was Perkins' brand-name syrup, which has the perfect balance of sweetness and maple-y tang and a consistency that fills the fat griddle squares with an ethereal vigor. Sounds heady, but it's true: prepping these waffles for devouring is as meditative as it is mouthwatering.

BEST

Waffle House's Waffle

Seems like a no-brainer that the house of waffles would have the best, but this yellow-signed beacon of breakfast glory isn't one to rest on its laurels of reputation. No, the waffles here are fresh, fluffy, but appropriately crispy and ready to melt pats of butter into their beckoning little squares. These are the waffles to start the day in that invigorating waffle way.

5

Breakfast Sides

Breakfast may seem simple, but the fact remains that the first meal of the day is all about idiosyncrasies. Much in the same way everyone these days has his or her own signature coffee drink (skinny, half-caf, two-pump vanilla, egg white iced Americano?), everyone has his or her own love affair with a certain breakfast side or two.

A side of this, a side of that … it's sides that really give a breakfast legs. What's a fluffy pancake without a side of moist, amber hash browns, after all? What's a scramble without a side of sausage? What's a waffle without a bowl of grits? What's a … well, you get the idea.

BAKED GOODS

GOOD

BETTER

Denny's Apple Pie

Rules are meant to be broken, and the one that says you can't have pie for breakfast was a dumb one anyway—especially when we're talking about a slice of apple pie from Denny's. Chasing bites of tender apples and flaky crust with sips of hot coffee could make the case for reinventing the shape of breakfast. Here's to hoping a piece of apple pie a day keeps the doctor away, too.

Bob Evans' Freshly Baked Buttermilk Biscuits

What more do you need to know? Bob Evans, a kingpin of Midwestern comfort foods, delivers a biscuit that amounts to the Rolls-Royce of flaky vehicles for buttery goodness. You'd be a fool not to put this one on your bucket list, but more foolish still would be not trying another slathered in Bob Evans' famous sausage gravy.

BEST

Perkins' Mammoth Muffin

A muffin so big and delicious it demands a trademark, the Mammoth Muffin makes a big, bold statement in a bakery known chiefly for its pies. Available in blueberry, apple-cinnamon, banana-nut, and a rotating chef's choice, this moist and delicious creation is great alongside any breakfast order or hoarded as part of a take-out order.

GOOD

Perkins' Smoked Kielbasa Sausage

This is a delicious smoked sausage with a different snap and spice than your average breakfast link. An integral part of the Hearty Man's Pancake Platter—alongside buttermilk pancakes, two eggs, smoked bacon, two sausage links, *and* a sausage patty—these smoky wonders often steal the show.

BETTER

Waffle House's Jimmy Dean Sausage

A breakfast name as big as Waffle House, Jimmy Dean makes a mean sausage patty, and putting these two giants together makes for a veritable morning dream team. The Jimmy Dean patties come in orders of two or three and make a fine companion to pretty much anything on the menu (even a large glass of Minute Maid orange juice).

BEST

Bob Evans' Sausage Patties

Sausage is so ubiquitous a breakfast staple that it's easy to take it for granted, but get your hands on a sausage patty from Bob Evans, and you'll quickly realize why these pucks are the stuff of legend. Lean and perfectly seasoned with a texture that arouses the palate, these patties are a crucible of morning sustenance.

GOOD

BETTER

Denny's Hash Browns

An invigorating balance of crispness and grease, the browns at Denny's remind you what potatoes are capable of. In this case, they're shredded nice and fine, and cooked until crisp and delicious.

Waffle House's Hash Browns

By themselves, these hash browns are good, but throw in a menagerie of toppings and additions— each with its own colorful lingo shouted by the wait-staff and line cooks—and you've got something better. Order them "chunked" (with diced ham), "peppered" (with diced jalapeño), "capped" (with grilled button mushrooms), or "smothered" (covered in sautéed onions)—or any way you like.

BEST

Waffle House's Grits

Chalk it up to Waffle House's southern roots (co-founders Joe Rogers and Tom Forkner opened the first in a suburb of Atlanta in 1955), but this chain knows its grits. They aren't soupy, and they aren't too dry. No, this finely attuned cornmeal is the perfect canvas for a slice of American cheese or a pat of butter and a dash of salt. (Or why not go with all three? You only live once.)

Serious About Grits
Grits are taken so seriously in the south, the South Carolina General Assembly wanted to make them an official state food.

PART

3

Appetizers and Salads

6

American Appetizers and Salads

Few may take the time to reflect on this, but the way you start a meal says a lot about you. They say the first step wins the race. Indeed, the first step you make—be it at a dinner table or a starting line—echoes symbolically through each initial maneuver you make in life.

Appetizers are a big deal, and one could convincingly argue that Americans invented some of the most amazing culinary creations of the twentieth century in this realm alone. In the new century, we're continuing to see improvements on such brilliant innovations as chicken tenders, spinach artichoke dips, and Tater Tots. The competition is stiff and rocketing toward the horizon, as you see from the following selections.

CAESAR SALAD

GOOD

BETTER

Applebee's Grilled Chicken Caesar Salad

This is a standout among standouts. Juicy, juicy, grilled, grilled chicken breast (pardon the stutter—it's that good!) on a bed of romaine in a garlic Caesar dressing. Challah croutons make this one a *mensch* among men (or, you know, salads).

Texas Roadhouse's Chicken Caesar Salad

The Roadhouse has done Julius proud with this take on the emperor's namesake salad. Romaine, not iceberg, is the key here—tossed up with housemade croutons, dressing with personality, and a heap of moist, grilled strips of chicken. Top that off with some Parmesan cheese, and you might not care about your entrée.

BEST

All Hail Caesar

The indispensable Caesar is widely believed to be the creation of Italian Chef Caesar Cardini, who came up with the recipe when his restaurant in Tijuana, Mexico, was rushed on July 4, 1924, and the kitchen was light on supplies. The chef's tableside preparation was added as dramatic flair, perhaps intended to distract from the slapdash origins of the dish.

Tony Roma's Caesar Salad

Straightforward and unbeatable. No, really—fresh romaine tossed with a lightly tangy Caesar dressing, crispy croutons, and shaved Asiago cheese is a combo that will make even salad-haters salivate. Add a fillet of salmon or breast of chicken, grilled or fried, and you can make a meal of what might otherwise be just a beginning.

GOOD

O'Charley's Chicken Tenders

Anybody can dish up some chicken, but O'Charley's knows how to dip and deep-fry better than most. Double-breading is the secret here, coupled with a kiss of sour buttermilk and the sweet-tang of honey mustard dressing. You're not just biting into fried batter; there's plenty of meat to go around.

BETTER

Shoney's Hand-Breaded Chicken Strips

Simple reigns supreme when it comes to these cluckers—juicy, tender morsels of all-white meat tucked into a batter somewhere between lacy and chip-crisp. Lather them in barbecue sauce, honey mustard, or ranch, and you're good to go.

BEST

Texas Roadhouse's Chicken Critters

The tenderest of the tender meets flakiest of the flaky in this crisp-of-the-crop recipe. Chicken tenders have never tasted so moist, so meaty, so … delicious. The signature batter plays second fiddle to none and makes these tenders a reason to stop by Texas Roadhouse just about every other meal. Accompanying steak fries only sweeten the deal.

CHICKEN WINGS

GOOD

Johnny Rockets' Rocket Wings

Stick to your roots, as they say. That's the Rocket Wings formula, anyhow—golden-fried, breaded, and served as you please with anything from bleu cheese to Hot Rocket Fuel. The glorious bit is, eat 'em plain and they're as good as anything soaked in hot sauce. Get a couple baskets of these, because you're going to be sharing them.

BETTER

Hooters' Chicken Wings

We all know Hooters is about one thing in particular, but in reality, they've got some dynamite wings to go with their … um … hooters. Ten hot sauces from mild to medium in flavors like Cajun and Parmesan Garlic means you can snack on your favorite while focusing on other things. Plus, if you plan on being around for a while, you can get 50 wings in one fell swoop.

BEST

Chili's Boneless Buffalo Wings

The best thing about these morsels of buffalo spicy goodness? They're boneless. That means nothing goes to waste—all the crispy batter and tender white chicken without a bone in sight. And for the faint of palate, there's bleu cheese dipping sauce to cool the tongue.

The Women of Hooters
The orange-beshorted, nude-pantyhosed enchantresses bringing those dynamite wings tableside aren't the only women in action at Hooters. A third of the management and corporate staff are also female (although only some of them get to wear whatever they want to work).

APPETIZERS & SALADS

GOOD

BETTER

Mimi's Cafe's Spinach and Artichoke Dip

Normally, this standby app draws you in with its creaminess, saltiness, and hint of spinach and artichoke. Look again: Mimi reinvents the classic with not one, not two, not three, but *four* cheeses and the rich-acidic character of sun-dried tomatoes. You might want to keep the dips to a healthy 15 to 20; there's an entrée coming, after all.

Chili's Skillet Queso

Need it be said that American comfort is bound up in cheese dips? Well, try this one on for size: seasoned ground beef (mmm), housemade salsa (spicy), and salty-feisty sizzling queso. You don't have to be watching a ball game to enjoy this skillet of deliciousness.

BEST

Nice and Cheesy
Can't get enough of Mimi's Cafe's Spinach and Artichoke Dip? The recipe is free for the following at mimiscafe.com. A warning to the heart healthy: this dip contains Parmesan, Swiss, and Jack cheeses plus a ½ cup Alfredo sauce.

Shoney's Spinach and Artichoke Dip with Dixie Tater Chips

This dream drench takes the basics—sautéed spinach, artichokes, and three different cheeses—and blends in that intangible streak of Shoney's TLC to deliver a dip fit to swim in. But wait, that's not all! You'll be scooping up mounds of this goodness with another Shoney's fave, the Dixie Tater Chips. These are crunchy salty platters perfect to escorting the royalty straight to your gullet.

GOOD

Red Robin's Kettle-Cooked Chips

What's so special about chips anyway? Start with slivers of potato, kettle-cook them until crunchy, sprinkle them with salt, and dish them up in a conical paper wrapping. But that's not where it ends. Order some Chili Con Queso, guac, and salsa, and start dipping to your heart's content. You'll never go back to a tortilla chip again.

BETTER

Applebee's Potato Twisters

Everybody loves a good chip-and-dip, but a twist now and then is a refresher to the palate. Hence the brilliant invention of Applebee's Potato Twisters—crispy, salty, piled high, and dished with a queso blanco rich with flavor. In case you needed more kick, tap the pico de gallo that it comes with. How's that for a twist?

BEST

Outback Steakhouse's Aussie Cheese Fries

The virtues of the Outback are indulgence and, well, indulgence. And there never was one more satisfying than a mound of thick-cut fries blanketed by melty Monterey Jack and cheddar cheeses plus bacon bits. Whether you eat it with a fork or dig in with your fingers, you probably won't stop until it's gone. Spicy ranch tags along, in case you need more flavor-punch per bite.

Got Tots?

Tater Tots had auspicious beginnings in the potato processing plant of the Grigg brothers, Nephi and Golden. Called Ore-Ida, as a nod to its location near the Oregon/Idaho border, the plant produced mountains of frozen french fries that created smaller mountains of scraps sold as cattle feed. That all changed when old Nephi had the idea of mixing the odds and ends with flour and spices, cutting them into nubs, and frying them, which in turn changed the way kids consumed tubers forever.

75

7

Asian Appetizers

In the realm of chain dining, Asian appetizers tend to be light and vibrant. Often imbued with citrus and soy, they are possessed of a certain levity that's harder to come by with other regional specialties. Plenty of fully greased Asian delights are also available, of course, but it's often the breezier fare that makes its way onto big restaurant menus, and the following pages.

This continuing selection of appetizers really does amount to the first page in a *Choose Your Own Adventure* book centered on creating a meal that's truly a journey. And really, who doesn't want to journey the vast culinary expanses of Asia?

CHICKEN SALADS

GOOD

BETTER

P.F. Chang's Chicken Chopped Salad

The Zen of healthy eating and firecracker flavor comes home to roost with this anything-but-boring healthy treat—chopped grilled chicken, fresh house greens, and your choice of toasty sesame dressing or feisty ginger dressing. Simple, but delicious—and there's no guilt involved.

The Cheesecake Factory's Chinese Chicken Salad

Toss out the ol' iceberg and ranch, and dive into an Eastern take on the salad—mandarin oranges, green onions, sliced almonds, sesame seeds, bean sprouts, rice noodles, and a sour-sweet Chinese plum dressing. There's enough texture and flavor to go around, and with these portions, you *will* be satisfied.

BEST

Mimi's Cafe's Asian Chopped Salad

This one's not only delightful for the palate, but for the eyes as well. A rainbow of cabbage, romaine, carrots, cilantro, green onions, and red and green bell peppers merge for a salad unlike anything you've yet enjoyed. Toss in some wontons for crunch and sesame dressing to round out the flavors, and you'll be dreaming of the flavors for weeks.

DUMPLINGS/POT STICKERS

GOOD

Mimi's Cafe's Asian Sampler

Although this impressive platter does justice to traditional Asian flavors, it's the pot stickers that really capture the taste buds. Perfectly steamed and not overseasoned, these glazed treats make a trip to Mimi's worth it—even if it's just for an appetizer or snack. The accompanying coconut shrimp and spicy chicken don't hurt either.

BETTER

The Cheesecake Factory's Pot Stickers

Adhering to the East's age-old methods, The Cheesecake Factory fills their pot stickers with delicious meat and spices and then pan-fries them. Simple but seductive. Served with soy-ginger sesame sauce, it's easy to eat several servings of these. If you're particularly addicted, order several and make it a full meal.

BEST

P.F. Chang's Dumplings

Chang's dumplings are second to none. Handmade daily and either pan-fried or steamed to your liking, these darlings are a perfect, bite-size taste of the East. Pick a spicy sauce for the dipping, and you'll find your mouth exploding with flavor. Nothing about this delightful app comes up short.

GOOD

P.F. Chang's Egg Rolls

Tradition reigns supreme when it comes to these egg rolls—and all of it with TLC. Hand-rolled and filled with flavorful, marinated pork and vegetables and then deep-fried to a perfect golden brown, these rolls come in pairs with sweet-and-sour and hot mustard dipping sauces for your pleasure. Simple is seductive, so be prepared to eat more than two.

BETTER

Bennigan's Southwest Egg Rolls

It's *West Side Story* in a roll. Sort of. Filled with egg, beans, Southwestern spices, chicken, and corn, one bite will have you rethinking the egg roll altogether. Top that with pineapple pepper cream sauce, and you have a creation that feeds outside the plate. You were expecting a little creativity with your meal, right?

BEST

California Pizza Kitchen's Tortilla Spring Rolls

Props to CPK for getting inventive with the tried-and-true. Who would have thought to offer fresh-from-the-oven tortilla spring rolls in varieties like Mediterranean, Baja, and Thai? That's fusion, folks. These toasty treats are just what the appetite ordered, treating you to mouthfuls of chicken, portobello mushrooms, cheese, peanut sauce, and guacamole—depending on which you order, of course.

LETTUCE WRAPS

GOOD

BETTER

Hard Rock Cafe's Chicken Lettuce Wraps

Starting with a canvas of crisp iceberg lettuce, wrap up your choice of marinated cucumber and red pepper salad, sweet matchstick carrots, bean sprouts, crisp fried wonton noodles, diced roast chicken breast, sautéed mushrooms, garlic, ginger, and toasted sesame seeds. Keep it all together, 'cuz you're going to want to dip this one in the Asian peanut and sweet-and-sour sauces.

P.F. Chang's Chang's Chicken Lettuce Wraps

Lettuce introduce you to the finest lettuce wrap this side of the ocean—P.F. Chang's own signature appetizer. It starts with wok-seared minced chicken and then wraps up mushrooms, green onions, and water chestnuts. It's all served over crispy rice sticks and served with cool, crisp lettuce cups. Salivating yet?

BEST

That's a Wrap!
A quick Google search brings up no fewer than 10 copycat recipes for P.F. Chang's Chicken Lettuce Wraps, proving they are indeed the stuff dreams are made of. Lettuce-wrapped dreams, that is.

The Cheesecake Factory's Thai Lettuce Wraps

DIY is all the rage—and not just when it comes to home improvement. Time to build your own app, as your taste buds dictate. Wrap up a personalized combo of satay chicken strips, carrots, bean sprouts, coconut curry noodles, and lettuce leaves and then dip in one … or two … or three delicious sauces: peanut, sweet red chili, and tamarind-cashew.

8

Italian Appetizers and Salads

Italian apps have a great way of highlighting the ingredients you'll likely find in your entrée. You just know the Roma tomatoes and olive oil in that bruschetta are going to make star turns elsewhere, as are the fresh basil and mozzarella in a caprese salad. Flatbread makes a great canvas for all manner of mouthwatering ingredients, including those beloved rings of calamari that are so good fried and dipped in spicy marinara.

In that way, Italian appetizers are like flipping through an interactive travel guide with lickable pages. No, that's not quite right. Let's say that appetizers of "the boot" are like smelling a loving Italian grandmother as she gives you a restorative hug. No? Maybe the only thing left to say is *mangia!*

BRUSCHETTA

GOOD

BETTER

Carino's Italian's Bruschetta

On the surface, you've seen one bruschetta, you've seen them all. But once you dig in and start crunching them, idiosyncrasies follow. Carino's lusty, crusty bread, for example, has the mellow tang of Roma tomatoes enlivened by a killer spiced olive oil. Let's not forget the zip of basil that makes this one a very good starter.

Buca di Beppo's Bruschetta

Bruschetta so good the pope can't say no. Okay, so that's not been verified, but it is a fact that Buca di Beppo's hearty slabs of toasted Italian bread are piled to delight with diced tomatoes, garlic-infused olive oil, basil, and Parmesan. Also, the large order is only $3 more than the small order, which makes the decision of how much a no-brainer.

BEST

Romano's Macaroni Grill's Tomato Bruschetta

Ah, Macaroni Grill, you bring us the pinnacle bruschetta experience— one alive with ripe grape tomatoes, fresh basil, garlic, and extra-virgin olive oil on grilled, rustic bread. All we can say is thank you for this mouthwatering appetizer that appetizes indeed. Also, thanks for the wine recommendation: Chianti D.O.C.G.

CALAMARI

GOOD

BETTER

Carino's Italian's Hand-Breaded Calamari

The secret to good calamari is that you get good calamari and you don't overcook them. Carino's has their recipe down-pat, and it's a sure thing you'll want to order it every time you come. Thin (but not chewy), breaded, and fried until golden, these babies make a glorious entrée into any meal—with a dip into spicy marinara, of course.

The Cheesecake Factory's Fried Calamari

For some, calamari have become mere canvases for dips and sauces—the french fries of the seafood world. Good to know some places still get it right. The Cheesecake Factory's calamari are indeed lightly fried, but they carry their own flavor and don't need to be sauced. That being said, it's still not a bad idea to taste a bit of the garlic dip with a bite or two.

BEST

Humble Beginnings
The first Buca di Beppo opened in the basement of a Minneapolis apartment building, which begs the question: how do you stop eating spicy calamari if it's always downstairs?

Buca di Beppo's Spicy Calamari

It's no wonder this Italian classic is one of the first temptations on Buca's menu—über tender, zestily breaded squid couple with a housemade marinara that's got just a bit of a kick. The great thing about this app is its abundant character—there's no doubt you're eating prime seafood, but calamari does tend to request a complement. With or without marinara, it's golden.

CAPRESE

GOOD

BETTER

Olive Garden's Caprese Flatbread

It's one thing when the classics are done with style, but it's quite another when the classics are revisited with pomp and circumstance. Give this twist of tradition a whirl: crispy-thin flatbread topped with the makings for a salty-vinegary-garlicky-sweet caprese salad. Toss in some fresh basil, and you might wow Italy's staunch culinarians.

Buca di Beppo's Mozzarella Caprese

Nothing packs a sweeter punch than vine-ripened tomatoes—precisely the ingredients of choice in this classic salad. But Italians know that while simple is best, you have to keep the ingredients top-notch. With that in mind, Buca drizzles on premium olive oil (only extra-virgin), slices tender-moist mozzarella, and layers it all with leaves of basil sweet from the plant. Buca ain't foolin'.

BEST

Romano's Macaroni Grill's Mozzarella Alla Caprese

Great caprese is no secret recipe; Macaroni Grill is well schooled in the virtues of Italian cooking, thereby producing a caprese salad second to none. All the ingredients are crème de la crème, but there's one addition that gives this dish a beautiful complexity: aged balsamic vinegar. We're talking salad taken to the next level.

GOOD

T.G.I. Friday's Spinach Florentine Flatbread

Flatbread is that catch-all, dull appetizer that's mostly just good as a vehicle for sauces and dips. Not at T.G.I. Friday's, however. Thank God it's Spinach Florentine—a creamy spinach and artichoke spread topped with a traditional bruschetta combination of tomatoes, garlic, and chopped basil. No shortage of flavor here.

BETTER

Tony Roma's Steak and Wild Mushroom Flatbread

One of Tony Roma's most popular starters, this crispy creation is reminiscent of pizza—bedecked with beef tenderloin, Havarti, bleu cheese, wild mushrooms, red peppers, chive, and creamy horseradish sauce. Sounds like a mouthful, huh? Chances are it will be several mouthfuls.

BEST

Olive Garden's Grilled Chicken Flatbread

Keeping it simple but always delicious, Olive Garden takes bruschetta to a new level with thin flatbread baked until golden and topped with grilled chicken, roasted red peppers, alfredo sauce, and garlic, making it the best you'll taste this side of "the boot." Top that off with a garlic spread to create even more zing, and bruschetta seems like … well, old news.

9

Mexican Appetizers

Sometimes it seems like Mexican food has an unfair advantage in the realm of appetizers. Guacamole is one of the best dips in the charted universe, nachos might be proof of the existence of God, and quesadillas are always giving pizza a run for the title of Best Flat Thing Bearing Cheese.

Need proof? Find a chain restaurant menu without at least one dish that bears the direct influence of Mexican cuisine. Mexican food is everywhere! Luckily, the best way to put this dominance to the test is to eat a whole bunch of food.

GUACAMOLE

GOOD

BETTER

Chili's Fire-Grilled Corn Guacamole

Good guacamole is like a quiet little party in your mouth—or at least it should be. Take Chili's version—jalapeños, cilantro, pico de gallo, fresh avocados, and fire-grilled corn kernels. Try fitting that on a chip, and another one, and another one, and another one ....

The Cheesecake Factory's Guacamole Made-to-Order

Not only are the offerings generous, but the ingredients in this Cheesecake Factory favorite are top-notch. Vet your chip with the likes of this unbeatable guac: fresh avocados, chiles for some kick, lime, and cilantro. It's all served up alongside crisp, flavorful chips—not those sad excuses for fried tortillas. Take it to the next level with housemade salsa and sour cream on the side.

BEST

Say What?
Avocados get their name from *ahuacatl*, the Aztec word for "testicle." It's not all clean and pretty out there, folks.

Ruby Tuesday's Fresh Guacamole Dip

Use the best, freshest ingredients, and you've got no competition. Ruby Tuesday plays it well with their housemade guacamole—a rich blend of buttery avocados, pico de gallo that offers a little kick, and fresh salsa. Then, of course, there are the delicious tortilla chips that come with no end—in case you were worried you had to start eating your guacamole with a spoon.

NACHOS

GOOD

BETTER

T.G.I. Friday's Tostado Nachos

Thank God it's … nachos. Tostado nachos, to be specific. With a mound of refried beans to lead, seasoned ground beef (that doesn't kick you in the tongue), the gentle punch of jalapeños, and salsa/sour cream to boot, this one's a good bet whatever the time of day.

Carino's Italian's Italian Nachos

Usually a food group dominated by Mexican flavors, Carino's doesn't hesitate to give us a new take on the standard with pepperoncini, mozzarella and Parmesan, black olives, and Roma tomatoes. Add to that chicken or sausage, and you've got a meal on a plate. (Just don't order the family size for yourself; it looks bad.)

BEST

Chili's Classic Nachos

Loaded 'chos are what it's about at Chili's—no skimping here. Prep your taste buds for the likes of melted cheddar, tangy-spicy jalapeños, beans, queso, and just the right amount of seasoned ground beef. Mix and dip with your own sides of housemade pico de gallo, and cool it down with sour cream. This one's bound to become a new American comfort food.

QUESADILLAS

GOOD

Perkins' Chick 'n Cheese Quesadilla

The quesadilla prides itself on being an unbeatable step up from the nacho. At Perkins, the quesadilla is a serious culinary endeavor—primed with Cajun-seasoned chicken (recalling the sass of New Orleans) and pepper Jack and cheddar cheeses, all grilled in a tomato tortilla. Eat this as seriously as it was prepared.

BETTER

Red Robin's Just-in-Quesadilla

The quesadilla isn't some shoddy afterthought at Red Robin; it's stuffed with juicy chicken, mushrooms, Jack and cheddar cheeses, freshly chopped cilantro, and tomatoes. Suffice it to say, it's a tortilla-wrapped fiesta. And in case you like adding your own flare, all the fixins are included—guacamole, salsa, black beans, and sour cream.

BEST

Ruby Tuesday's California Club Quesadilla

Trust us when we say Ruby Tuesday's quesadilla is no shameful combo of American cheese between stale tortillas. Take the prime-choice California Club—tender grilled chicken, tomatoes, and bacon enveloped by gooey cheddar and Swiss cheeses, all between two fresh tortillas, straight from the griddle.

10

Seafood Appetizers

There's no use trying to put lipstick on this pig: seafood isn't the strong suit of our nation's great chain restaurants. That isn't to say that when it's done it isn't done well, but the options are often a touch limited. You're not going to find fresh steamed periwinkle snails on Chili's menu anytime soon.

This makes sense, as keeping seafood fresh is always a challenge, and the ocean's bounty can be a bit unpredictable—unpredictability being the great nemesis of consistency. Still, there's enough booty to make delicious work of. Even if it's just for the first course.

GOOD

BETTER

The Cheesecake Factory's Crabcakes

Done the old-fashioned American way, these flaky numbers get a taste of life by the sea. That is, they're just what you'd expect from the coast of Maine—moist and tender inside, crispy outside. Instead of embellishing the perfect cake with overspiced sauces, The Cheesecake Factory chooses a classic: tartar sauce. There's no going wrong there.

Red Lobster's Pan-Seared Crab Cakes

It stands to reason that Red Lobster would dish up some delish cakes, but dig what makes these extra special: the Holy Trinity. That's right, celery, onion, and bell peppers mix with premium crabmeat to produce this dynamite cake—and you get a pair of them. Gently top with a dollop of rémoulade for creaminess and kick, and you've got a party in your mouth.

BEST

Ruby Tuesday's Jumbo Lump Crab Cake

Both a healthy snack and a delicious indulgence, these tender, moist treats remind you what every crab cake should be about—delicious crab, that is. Seared until golden brown for the perfect texture, these cakes are perfect paired with spicy chile sauce. Who knew you could be satisfied with only 366 calories?

GOOD

BETTER

P.F. Chang's Seared Ahi Tuna

This is as simple as it comes, pure as the sea: sushi-grade ahi tuna, dished up with a flavorful mustard vinaigrette and laid on a bed of fresh mixed greens. The focus here is the fish, so be prepared to muster your taste buds for an experience that pays due homage to ahi's rare and elegant form.

The Cheesecake Factory's Ahi Carpaccio

Yes, there are more than 200 items on The Factory's menu, but that doesn't mean they don't do things right. Take the Ahi Carpaccio, for instance— thin slices of raw ahi tuna coupled with wasabi pesto for kick, creamy avocado to soothe, and tograshi aioli … just because it's awesome. Don't overlook this gem the next time you're surfing for an app.

BEST

Outback Steakhouse's Seared Ahi Tuna

You wouldn't expect flavors this bold (and Asian) to come from the same place as the Bloomin' Onion and Fosters. Brace yourself: this sashimi-style tuna is rubbed in self-professed bold spices, seared rare, and served with creamy ginger-soy and a kick-in-the-pants wasabi vinaigrette.

GOOD

BETTER

Ruby Tuesday's Thai Phoon Shrimp

The play on words is as good as the play in your mouth—deep-fried, battered shrimp nudge up against a sweet chile sauce that makes for a fiery-sweet indulgence. Not for the faint of heart, these darlings are just one of those appetizers you can't live without.

Red Lobster's Parrot Isle Jumbo Coconut Shrimp

Take a tropical dip with these fried delights—nothing quite like a battered, tender shrimp rolled in coconut and an out-of-this-hemisphere piña colada dip to tease your tongue. They're a favorite for a reason.

BEST

P.F. Chang's Dynamite Shrimp

Ever the balance of spicy and mild, cooling and hot, P.F. Chang's wows with their unassuming Dynamite Shrimp, a study in contrasts—tender inside, crispy outside, tossed in zesty sauce, and laid on a bed of cool cabbage and rice sticks. These are an indulgence you're guaranteed to come back to.

Bill Darden
Red Lobster was founded in 1968 by Bill Darden, who opened his first restaurant, The Green Frog, when he was 19. Darden Restaurants is now the world's biggest restaurant company, boasting more than 680 Red Lobster locations, plus scads of Olive Garden, LongHorn Steakhouse, and The Capital Grille outposts worldwide.

APPETIZERS & SALADS

Sandwiches

11

Hot Sandwiches

Abraham Lincoln, Winston Churchill, John Montagu—history is littered with great men and great achievements, but it's the legacy of the latter that has the most enduring grip on our daily life. True, if Lincoln hadn't won the Civil War for the North, we'd be looking at a very different chain-restaurant landscape. And if Churchill hadn't done his part in securing an Allied victory in World War II, we might be eating nothing but schnitzel. But if Montagu, the fourth Earl of Sandwich, hadn't commanded his servants to bring him slices of meat between slices of bread so he could stay at the gaming table with one hand free, we'd be having a devil of a time texting and lunching at the same time.

Part of America's rich lunch heritage, the hot sandwich has manifested in everything from French Dip to Grilled Chicken, with iterations everywhere in between that boggle the mind. There's no telling where the next generation of America's culinary dear will lead—but these are a few of the prized creations that will get you salivating ... and inspired.

GOOD

O'Charley's Prime Rib Philly

This indulgence makes Philly's beloved sandwich a little uneasy—if only because it's prime competition for sammys made in Philadelphia itself. Try this on for size: thinly sliced, slow-roasted prime rib with sautéed mushrooms, caramelized onions, peppers, and spicy queso. It's all served up on a hoagie with a grin. Just don't tell Philly she's giving the genuine article a run for its money.

BETTER

Applebee's Slow-Simmered Beef Sandwich

Ever thought the endless charade of sides could be consolidated into one sandwich? So did Applebee's. Here you've got one sandwich with a boatload of ingredients— including tender beef, jalapeño coleslaw, crispy onion rings, and sweet-and-hot sauce made in-house. It's not a question of whether or not to eat; it's a question of how.

BEST

Phantastic Philly

Everyone knows a genuine Philly cheesesteak is made with nothing more than steak, a hoagie, and Cheez Whiz. Unless, of course, you make it with provolone. And you add onions. And peppers. Maybe some hot sauce. Or ketchup. And mayo— definitely mayo.

Logan's Roadhouse's Steak Melt

Where else would you find the finest hot beef sandwich but in the halls of a great steak house? To wit: Logan's presents theirs with grilled sirloin, provolone, sautéed mushrooms, and Brewski Onions. Lest the bun be an afterthought, they made it a forethought—it all starts with a ciabatta canvas. You were in need of some red meat, right?

CHICKEN

GOOD

T.G.I. Friday's Jack Daniel's Chicken Sandwich

The chicken king's savory favorite is no secret—whoever the chicken king is. T.G.I. Friday's has him satiated with a Jack Daniel's–glazed breast, bacon, cheeses galore, Cajun onion straws, and more Jack Daniel's in the form of a lusty mayo. It's all a bit scrumptious on a brioche bun, wouldn't you say?

BETTER

California Pizza Kitchen's California Club Sandwich

What makes it a California Club? Ask Wolfgang Puck. Really, all that matters is that it's irresistible. Who else could take chicken, applewood-smoked bacon, avocado, and the usual fixins to such a level? It helps, of course, that it's accompanied by gracious herb-cheese focaccia and soup or salad—depending on your appetite.

BEST

Mimi's Cafe's Monterey Chicken Burger

Who ever said the burger demanded beef patties? Mimi's knows better, dishing up this ooey-gooey treat with melted Jack, broiled chicken breast, smoky bacon, avocado, and the ingenious kicker— pesto aïoli. Who cares if you order fries with a sandwich like this? Your appetite won't even make it that far.

Gentleman Jack
Jack Daniel has often been known to serve breast of chicken with whiskey sauce at his ranch in Tennessee. He enjoys this at the head of an oak table while sipping a glass or two of Gentleman Jack.

SANDWICHES

PORK

GOOD

Cracker Barrel's BLT

Here's a taste of tradition in a sandwich—but nothing overwrought and certainly not boring. Eating bacon is America's favorite pastime, but when you add that to a sourdough-hugged sammy piled with fresh tomatoes and crisp lettuce, you've got a winning meal in your hands. Here at the Barrel, BLTs come with fixins— coleslaw and soup or steak fries, that is.

BETTER

Chili's BBQ Pulled Pork Sandwich

Holy hog, is this one delicious sandwich. Tender, moist, meaty pulled pork slides into a sesame seed bun (or wheat, if you prefer) and rests beneath a mound of those delectable, deep-fried, crispy onion rings. Housemade barbecue sauce and a heaping mound of crunchy-sweet coleslaw smacks of good eats any time of day.

BEST

Mimi's Cafe's French Quarter

Calling to mind the wafting smells and unceasing bustle of New Orleans, this sandwich is rife with crispy bacon, fresh avocado, a king's helping of Swiss, dressing of 1,000 Islands, and all the usual accoutrements on top of garlic-Parmesan bread. It's a mouthful in size and character worthy of the undertaking.

French Quarter
Le Vieux Carré, or French Quarter, in New Orleans is home to many a fascination, including Spanish-style architecture from previous Spanish rule, Jackson Square, licentious Bourbon Street, and the inimitable Café du Monde, which deep-fries beignets and pours out coffee 24 hours a day.

SANDWICHES

VEGETARIAN

GOOD

The Cheesecake Factory's Grilled Cheese

Never think the grilled cheese is relegated to the bedside on sick days—this dynamo is as robust and fulfilling 365 days a year. Delicious melted on egg bread here at The Factory, you get to choose the kind of cheese that pleases. Feel free to pair with a salad or fries, but it's recommended that you consider a soup to complement this classic.

BETTER

Hooters' Grilled Cheese Platter

Now, now don't go thinking Hooters is all about … hooters. The sandwiches are nothing to wag your ketchup-glazed fingers at. In fact, the Grilled Cheese Platter is worth a second bite—and a third, and fourth, and fifth. It helps that a curly fry side is hard to dig up nowadays. Easy eating if your attention is, well, elsewhere.

Humble Eats

Grilled cheese began humbly at the start of the Great Depression as an easy source of cheap food—American cheese and mediocre white bread. Nothing more. Remember that come April when we celebrate Grilled Cheese Month by eating 30 different kinds of grilled cheese sandwiches.

BEST

California Pizza Kitchen's Grilled Vegetable Sandwich

Yes, CPK is mostly about pizza, but they don't skimp on the sandwiches. Case in point: their vegetable variety. This one's about serious portobellos, grilled up with bell peppers and mounded on focaccia with sun-dried tomato aïoli. Per expectation, the sides are apt pairs: soup or salad (your choice of Caesar salad or Szechuan slaw).

12
Cold Sandwiches

It's best not to get distracted by the metaphorical implications of this chapter being sandwiched between appetizers and entrées, for sandwiches hold court no matter where they appear. It's a trick they learned from their father, old Montagu, who held court of office for more than 50 years. That's just a drop in the pond compared to the legacy of his favorite snack, which seems likely to dominate the midday for another 50 years at least, which leads us to the cold sandwich.

The centerpiece of any good picnic—heck, any decent lunch—the cold sandwich shares notoriety with all the great American dishes but holds a special place in our hearts. Its casual comfort and easy preparation make it always accessible, while its versatility fires our imaginations. Start with a club and go from there—in today's culinary world, the sky's the limit (and you surely have Montagu's blessing).

GOOD

BETTER

Cracker Barrel's Chicken Salad Sandwich

Salad in a sandwich? Take a second gander: creamy chicken salad on Cracker Barrel's famed sourdough with sides of your choosing and flavor that leaves your taste buds tickled with delight. It's tried and it's true, but it's something new, too—turned, of course, into a platter ripe for lunching.

Shoney's Chicken Salad Croissant Sandwich

Everyone loves a warm, buttery, flaky croissant. But Shoney's has taken that deliciousness to an exciting new level by pairing it with chicken salad—that is, chunks of tender chicken, toasted pecans, seedless grapes, and crisp celery. This is one salad that's never short on flavor or texture—a beautiful crunch that satisfies even the pickiest chicken salad sandwich lovers.

Good Marketing

Chicken salad has a history dating to 1863, when MacGyver of the kitchen Liam Gray mixed together some leftovers and sold it at Town Meats in Wakefield, Rhode Island. Goes to show you can sell anything with good marketing.

BEST

Mimi's Cafe's Turkey Pesto Ciabatta

Piled high with freshly roasted turkey breast, this ciabatta-tastic treat sports creamy pesto, fresh tomato and avocado, and silky-smooth mozzarella. This sammy has the perfect balance of texture and flavor, so if you weren't hungry before, you will be now.

SEAFOOD

GOOD

BETTER

Red Lobster's Crunch Fried Fish Sandwich

In this Red Lobster staple, toasted sourdough lays a tangy foundation for a fillet of deep-fried goodness. Top that off with some melted Jack, and pair it with house-cooked potato chips, and you've got yourself one heck of a meal. The only things missing are an ice cold beer and good company.

Mimi's Cafe's Albacore Salad and Avocado Sandwich

Here are some curious bedfellows: albacore and avocado. They have more than their first letters in common, don't you know. A rich cheddar cheese plays up the avocado while the tenderness of the albacore gives you pause—only long enough to take a breath before your next delicious bite.

BEST

Tasty Tuna
Also known as tuna, albacore is often cooked in "steak" form, or canned in oil or water for enjoyment in tuna salads, tuna bakes, tuna casseroles, or with your fingers in a dark kitchen after midnight when you can't sleep.

Red Lobster's New England Lobster Rolls

New England's got the original, but these are a fair game for a fair price. Maine lobster meat (is there any better?) is tossed with creamy mayo, celery, and onion and nudged into two buttery rolls. No fuss, no complications—just the real thing, done right. Oh, it's best to enjoy this happy sammy with a light brew or two.

GOOD

BETTER

Shoney's Turkey Club

Self-dubbed the Colossus of Shoney's, this big treat sports roasted turkey, hickory-smoked bacon, American and Swiss cheeses, and grilled sourdough to top it off. It's about the ingredients here, and they speak for themselves. And they'll linger in your memory long after the meal is over.

Bennigan's Turkey O'Toole

A couple neat little twists to this sammy make it a welcome change from the ordinary. Try this on for size: roasted turkey breast, Swiss cheese, and smoky-sweet Dijon dressing—all served up on a pretzel bun. When you think about it, it's really just an ingenious take on a stuffed pretzel. Who wouldn't want to try that?

BEST

The Cheesecake Factory's The Club

Now, it's common knowledge that chicken holds the place of honor on a club—or does it? Not so anymore. Think freshly roasted turkey breast, bacon, lettuce, tomato, mayonnaise, and flavorful toasted bread to round out the club sandwich for the new age. Sure, it's been done, but has it ever been done this well?

1-800-BUTTERBALL
The Butterball Turkey Talk-Line is open during November and December for all your pressing turkey-roasting questions.

PART

5

Entrées

13

American
Entrées

Cue "Stars and Stripes Forever."

Speech begins: "My fellow Americans, this … is …
America. That's right. These are the dishes that have
made our nation one of renown, and occasionally scorn.
But haters beware, these are entrées that should never be
underestimated, for they have the power to comfort any
man, woman, or child from any culture anywhere.

"A bold claim, perhaps. But bold is what we're all about.
Few places give such ample evidence of our belly-busting,
big-hearted bravado as our nation's esteemed chain
restaurants. For it is in their hallowed halls that we enjoy
these entrées without guilt or guile. We enjoy them as
purely as anything can be enjoyed in the flicker of a life.
So without further ado, I say to you, *let's eat!*"

BEEF

GOOD

BETTER

T.G.I. Friday's Flat Iron

You never can go wrong with Black Angus, and T.G.I. Friday's is a case in point: 8 ounces of premium red meat fire-grilled until the perfect char paired with the perfect juiciness. Dished up with butter melting on top and whatever sides you think can stand up to such a regal cut, the Flat Iron deserves a gold star. Or maybe just your undivided attention.

The Cheesecake Factory's Hibachi Steak

Although this doesn't include the usual hibachi show, it does mean satisfaction: angus hanger steak (particularly tender) is dished up Eastern-style with meaty shiitake mushrooms, onions, bean sprouts, and—here's the kicker—wasabi mashed potatoes. Points for creativity, Cheesecake.

BEST

Outback Steakhouse's Special

Taking the gold in beef—because it *is* what's for dinner—Outback plays no tricks with its house signature cut. Signature spices (with a bold, savory kick) are all it needs before searing on a red-hot grill. Whatever you order as a side, be sure not to take the pomp and circumstance away from that first cut of meat.

ENTRÉES

GOOD

BETTER

Hard Rock Cafe's S.O.B. Burger

In case you needed proof Hard Rock has the (burger) stuff, look no further than the S.O.B. Burger. Spicy chipotle pepper purée couples with guacamole, green onions, and Jack cheese in this lusciously moist burger that can't possibly have an equal.

T.G.I. Friday's Kansas City BBQ Burger

It's the black angus that'll tickle your tongue the T.G.I.-way. Well, that and the Jack Championship Barbecue Sauce. And the applewood-smoked bacon. And the New York cheddar. And the onion strings. And—oh just order it already.

BEST

Red Robin's Bleu Ribbon Burger

This one's a winner—and a mouthful. Layers upon layers of goodness tower in this creation, including tomato, lettuce, onion, crumbled bleu cheese, crispy onion straws, and spicy chipotle mayo. Don't forget, of course, that Red Robin dishes up bottomless fries and service with a smile.

Genghis Burgers

Some historians trace the hamburger's beginnings to Mongolia, when Genghis Khan's men would ride with fistfuls of meat between their saddles and the backs of their horses. Tenderized during long journeys, these early burgers were eaten raw by famished soldiers on the move and pressed for time. The hamburger has truly come a long way.

ENTRÉES

CHICKEN

GOOD

Olive Garden's Stuffed Chicken Marsala

Why, old Italy would be proud. Tradition is here in full force, but not without notes of new-age twist: think creamy marsala sauce, tender mushrooms, oven-roasted chicken breast, and—the kicker—a stuffing of Italian cheese and sun-dried tomatoes. Even Grandma would be proud of that.

BETTER

Tony Roma's BBQ Half Chicken

Sure, Tony is known for his finger-lickin' ribs, but don't give him short shrift when it comes to this standby. Inexplicably juicy, lathered in Tony's Original sauce (à la BBQ), and charbroiled, this stick-to-your-ribs meal is anything but secondary in the Tony Roma's canon. In fact, it might just surpass a steak.

BEST

Texas Roadhouse's Smothered Chicken

This tasty treat is a marvel of indulgence. First, the folks at the Roadhouse marinate the chicken breast for flavor and tenderness, then they sauté onions and mushrooms, then they take no small step for foodie-kind: gravy. Oh, and there's Jack cheese in there, too. You might even request a bib, just in case.

GOOD

BETTER

Chili's Crispy Chicken Crispers

Think fried chicken in miniature. These white-meat treats are juicy-sweet and of course, covered in prime, crispy coating. Second only to the Colonel, they pair well with a mound of house fries and corn on the cob. Dipping sauces are a temptation, but consider the crisper on its own—standalone delicious.

Cracker Barrel's Fried Chicken Tenderloin

America's palate is tempted by a lot of things, but nothing more than juicy fried chicken. Cracker Barrel dishes up some of the best—bone free, served alongside tender, buttery buttermilk biscuits and some hearty veggies. If you're really adventurous, you might even ask for a helping of gravy.

BEST

Big Boy's Fried Chicken

It's greasy. It's meaty. It's delicious. Three pieces of heaven on a plate, golden and crispy, are all you need to sing satisfied. Before you get too excited about the chicken, though, remember there are two sides to sweeten the deal—like loaded mashed potatoes and green beans with bacon, maybe?

ENTRÉES

GOOD

BETTER

Shoney's Baked Spaghetti

"Spaghetti ladled with our rich tomato and meat sauce." Shoney's gets it—sauce needs to be *ladled*. The word suggests nothing but motherly love, for mothers love to ladle. Here, the ladling is followed by a trip to the oven so the mozzarella cheese on top can get all brown and gooey. Thanks, Mom—er, Shoney's.

Village Inn's Chicken Parmesan

What could be better for the weary traveler than wandering into a village at dusk and finding a steaming plate of penne pasta topped with breaded, baked chicken, and cascading rivulets of marinara waiting at the friendly inn? This fantasy becomes piping-hot reality at Village Inn, where Chicken Parmesan is everything Old World and always a comfort.

BEST

Cracker Barrel's Mac 'n' Cheese

This comfort food is totally rich and creamy, complete with breadcrumb topping, just like Grandma made it. That's pretty much standard operating procedure at Cracker Barrel: down-home cooking that's satisfying and rib-sticking. Dig in.

ENTRÉES

PORK

GOOD

BETTER

Romano's Macaroni Grill's Pan-Roasted Pork Chop

You might not often think of ordering a pork chop at a pasta haven like Macaroni Grill, but think again: a juicy pork chop saddles up next to fresh pea and mushroom risotto and is dished up with an eminently flavorful Chianti-mustard sauce. *Delicioso!*

Texas Roadhouse's Grilled Pork Chops

The staple of the South—and the Midwest, and the East, and anywhere pork is king—finds a home at Texas Roadhouse. Here, boneless, hand-cut chops are grilled until tender and served with peppercorn sauce for kick. Don't you worry about the pork chop's curse—sawdust dryness. This here is the real (juicy) thing.

BEST

Outback Steakhouse's Sweet Glazed Pork Tenderloin

Hearty and homey, just like you'd expect of the Outback, the pork sings sweet tunes during its slow-roasting, given a bit of zip to counter the sweet. Garlic mashed potatoes (is there any other kind?) and al dente green beans follow as entourage, not to be outdone by the tender, moist pork that steals the spotlight.

ENTRÉES

GOOD

BETTER

Ruby Tuesday's Classic Barbecue Baby-Back Ribs

It's no secret, really—ribs need the TLC of homemade barbecue sauce and slow-roasting until fork-tender. A happy compromise between meaty and tangy, these ribs will stick to your ribs with pleasure. Top them off with a signature cheesy biscuit, and you'll be singing Ruby's praises all the way home.

Chili's Shiner Bock BBQ Ribs

Ribs are like a good bowl of chili—everyone has his or her own recipe. Turns out, though, this recipe is one of the best. Beer-spiked barbecue sauce slathers house-smoked ribs to render a tender, juicy, meaty meal that just doesn't compare. Home-style fries and cinnamon apples, to boot? Well now, they're just showing off.

BEST

LongHorn Steakhouse's Baby Back Ribs

Maybe it's the barbecue sauce, rich and feisty. Or maybe it's the ribs and their tender, fall-off-the-bone meat. Or maybe it's, well, everything. It's hard to pinpoint what makes this king of ribs feast such an addictive entrée, but why spoil the mystery? Half rack or full, there's no beating LongHorn's succulent ribs.

Bodacious BBQ

It's widely believed that the word *barbecue* comes from the American and Caribbean Indian word *barabicu,* which means "sacred fire pit." This is totally in line with the attitude many of the most ardent pit masters have about the sacred superiority of their specific barbecue setup. It also readily extends the religious fervor with which barbecue enthusiasts pledge allegiance to the barbecue styles of certain regions (i.e., Kansas City versus St. Louis). Sauciness, it would seem, is next to godliness.

ENTRÉES

GOOD

BETTER

Mimi's Cafe's Pistachio Crusted Salmon

Whodathunk? Pistachios and fish? Oh yes. That earthy, salty, sweet of pistachios makes the perfect cover for flaky salmon and sits nicely atop a rustic artichoke ragout alongside fresh vegetables. A nice pilaf completes the indulgence, made only the more perfect in good company.

Red Lobster's Ultimate Feast

Well now, not to be greedy, but don't you want to sample a little bit of everything? That is, a little bit of the best of everything? Like, oh, split Maine lobster, for instance? And steamed snow crab legs? And garlic shrimp scampi? And Walt's Favorite Shrimp? And … well that's enough for one meal, don't you think?

BEST

The Cheesecake Factory's Jamaican Black Pepper Shrimp

This one's not for the faint of palate, but no one said delicious was easy. Sauté fresh shrimp with *hotttt* Jamaican pepper sauce, and cut it with some fried plantains and cool mango salsa. Rice and black beans are a nice touch—why you can even add chicken to the mix if you're feeling particularly peckish.

ENTRÉES

VEGETARIAN

GOOD

BETTER

California Pizza Kitchen's Pear and Gorgonzola Pizza

Sound a little too frou-frou for you-you? Put your hang-ups in check because Bosc pears along with Gorgonzola, Fontina, and mozzarella cheeses do amazing things with caramelized onions and hazelnuts on this elegant piece of 'zartistry. It's topped with field greens tossed in Gorgonzola ranch, for good measure.

Red Robin's Classic Creamy Mac 'n' Cheese

Just because you're forgoing meat doesn't mean you can't indulge a little—or, in this case, a lot, with an entrée-size serving of macaroni and cheese. Cavatappi pasta is tossed in a velvet four-cheese sauce, topped with more yummy cheese, and baked to golden brown. Served with warm garlic focaccia bread and a side salad? Oh, I think so.

BEST

Applebee's Spinach and Artichoke Dip

Odds are, if you're a vegetarian in a chain restaurant, you're there for the spinach and artichoke dip, so why not go with one that's famous. Mmmmm, yes: a warm crock of creamy spinach, tender artichoke hearts, and melted Asiago and Parmesan cheeses ... oh, and a spicy chipotle lime salsa. Ready those tortilla chips!

ENTRÉES

14

Asian Entrées

In Asia, entrées are a subjective experience, mostly because defining a cuisine as something as broad and formless as Asian can be difficult. Still, to break down the cuisines of so many distinct regions and cultures—China, Korea, Cambodia, Thailand, Vietnam, Indonesia, the Philippines, India, Sri Lanka, are all part of Asia—would be more than a little maddening if your endgame is nothing more than a delicious serving of teriyaki shrimp and noodles (which is Japanese, by the way).

Like so many American melting pots, chain restaurants evolve in response to popular tastes, and as our population continues getting a broader picture of the world via their taste buds, expect the menus to provide a tasty reflection. So without further ado, a journey into the unknown … into the eminently unknowable ….

GOOD

BETTER

The Cheesecake Factory's Crispy Spicy Beef

This is texture heaven. Never devoid of flavor, strips of beef are sautéed with green beans, shiitake mushrooms, onions, carrots, and a touch of sesame seeds. Lather that (carefully, mind you) with sweet-and-sour sauce. It's no wonder The Cheesecake Factory is known for more than just cakes made of cheese.

P.F. Chang's Beef à la Sichuan

Flank steak beats strip steak. At least it does in this quasi-Vietnamese dish. Strips of flavorful flank steak are cooked until crispy and then tossed with julienned carrots and celery. Not only is it a kick for spice lovers, but its simplicity gives the steak the well-earned spotlight.

BEST

T.G.I. Friday's Japanese Hibachi Skewers

Black angus sirloin makes its entry with much fanfare: marinated in garlic, black pepper, and soy sauce, grilled to your preference, and garnished with sesame seeds. Oh, it's also dished up with ginger-lime slaw and some grilled pita. It's particularly attractive because the whole dish clocks in at under 750 calories.

GOOD

BETTER

O'Charley's Teriyaki Sesame Chicken

It's hot, it's rich, it's sweet, it's savory, it's … Teriyaki Sesame Chicken. Carefully cut strips of chicken lay down with mushrooms, peppers, and onions, fired by chiles, sesame-pineapple sauce, and the ever-popular teriyaki. Just in case it's a little too feisty for you, it's dished up with a taming bed of rice.

P.F. Chang's Sesame Chicken

Sure, it's that staple for westerners craving Asian fare, but it's so often oversweet, poorly breaded, and sawdusty. Not here. Juicy white meat chicken is gently coated, crispy-fried, and tossed with broccoli, onions, and red bell peppers in a spicy sesame sauce. Num num.

BEST

**The Cheesecake Factory's
Orange Chicken**

It's got just the right
amount of zest, you know?
Deep-fried premium
chicken meets sweet-
and-spicy orange sauce
accompanied by white
rice and a medley of
fresh vegetables. Never
oversauced, these are the
real thing: bright, bold,
daring, and full of just the
right kind of flavor.

ENTRÉES

GOOD

California Pizza Kitchen's Kung Pao Spaghetti

Who goes to CPK and doesn't order pizza? You might, if you knew what they had in store: fire-cracked Kung Pao with that halting aroma of garlic and green onions, the crunch of peanuts, and the kick of red chiles. Enjoy with chicken, shrimp, or both, but never pigeonhole CPK again.

BETTER

Applebee's Teriyaki Shrimp Pasta

It's a take on an Italian classic—sort of. Freshness, crunch, and flavor meld well in the bowl as you chomp down on bok choy, sugar snap peas, water chestnuts, mushrooms, and grilled shrimp. It's all tossed in a not-too-sweet teriyaki sauce and topped with cilantro. The best part? It's a guilt-free indulgence at under 550 calories.

BEST

P.F. Chang's Double Pan-Fried Noodles Combo

Quite a mouthful, eh? And the name is only the beginning. Crispy egg noodles are stir-fried with mushrooms, bok choy, carrots, celery, onions, and—wait for it—a combination of beef, pork, chicken, and shrimp. If you're hungry after licking your bowl, there's something wrong with you.

ENTRÉES

GOOD

BETTER

Applebee's Sizzling Asian Shrimp

How does Applebee's do Asian, you ask? The answer: with the same blend of flavor and fun in the form of sizzling shrimp atop a skillet overflowing with rice, broccoli, red peppers, sugar snap peas, water chestnuts, mushrooms, carrots, and bok choy. There's even some cilantro on top!

The Cheesecake Factory's Miso Salmon

Sushi is exciting and all, but Japan's more revelatory export—for those tracking such things—is miso. A healthful fermented paste made from any number of sources (including rice, barley, and most familiarly, soy). The result is savory, salty, and just a little sweet, making it the perfect coating for a tender fillet of salmon. Hats off to The Cheesecake Factory for this one.

BEST

Here's to Hunan
The three trademarks of Hunan cuisine are its fiery flavors, enticing aromas, and deep colors. Dishes are often stewed, fried, pot-roasted, braised, or smoked.

P.F. Chang's Hunan-Style Hot Fish

You've been served plenty of evidence supporting the power of consistency, but it's always nice to find a surprise here and there, which is precisely why this dish wins "best." Crispy slices of fresh fish—a daily selection—in a tangy, spicy sauce with stir-fried vegetables. Simple stuff, but the potential for variety scrapes rarefied air in these, our comfy quarters.

GOOD

P.F. Chang's Coconut Curry Vegetables

Filling without skimping on flavor, this medley boasts silken tofu, peanuts for texture, and a gentle curry powder that gives the dish depth and character. Toss that with coconut milk sauce, set aside a bed of white rice, and you have a meal. While you can certainly rejoice in a dish you'll come back for, it's also very healthy for you. Cheers to that!

BETTER

The Cheesecake Factory's Thai Salad

Usually this dish includes chicken, but it's just as tasty without—a blend of freshly julienned carrots, green onions, and a spicy peanut sauce (that really makes the dish). Toss that with linguini and bean sprouts for a tasty treat that satisfies both vegetarians and carnivores.

BEST

P.F. Chang's Stir-Fried Eggplant

It sounds simple, but this dish rocks in the character department. Picture it: Chinese eggplant (a particularly flavorful variety) is tossed with chili paste and scallions for kick. Served with a side of rice, you can set your mouth on fire with a bite of eggplant and then happily quench the flames.

15

Cajun/Creole Entrées

The culinary releases of the bayou rank right up there with the musical exports in terms of flavor and influence. That's right, Satchmo, Dixieland jazz is just as bright and craveable as jambalaya. None of this has been lost on the esteemed corporate chefs underneath toques in the test kitchens of our beloved chain restaurants.

As with most cuisines, there are central ingredients to this way of cooking, rice perhaps chief among them. And of course you can't go anywhere Cajun without the holy trinity: celery, peppers, and onion (insert obligatory *oh-knee-yon* joke here). But those are just the foundation ingredients. Myriad spices are ready to go berserk on a whole kaleidoscope of meat, fish, and poultry. Satisfaction *gare-ohn-teed*.

GOOD

BETTER

Mimi's Cafe's Top Sirloin

While it's true that Cajun country doesn't dip into beef much, this is a fine example of why they should: a delectable, juicy cut rubbed with Cajun spices and pan-seared for a near-blackened flavor, full of pizzazz. Dished up with veggies of your choosing and of course a baked potato, this is one beef dish that hits home.

Shoney's 12-Ounce T-Bone, Blackened

It's hard to find a good piece of meat, and harder still to find good meat seasoned to perfection. In case you were wondering, Shoney's T-bone is a model to follow: choose it blackened and medium-rare. Served with a baked potato and a fair amount of due pride, this is one entrée that won't leave you wanting.

BEST

The Cheesecake Factory's Grilled Rib-Eye

Well, yes you can do this one up the standard, boring way—what with nothing but grilled marks and a touch of pink. But why not request the Cajun rendition, bursting with the flavors of the South? It's marinated for 36 hours in just the right combination of herbs and spices, so there's definitely a mouthful of flavor.

ENTRÉES

GOOD

BETTER

The Cheesecake Factory's Cajun Chicken Littles

Don't be fooled by the quaint name; these spicy chicken pieces are eminently satisfying. Uniquely spiced, breaded, and fried crisp, they're moist on the inside, crunchy on the outside, and served with the only accompaniments possible—mashed potatoes and glorious fresh corn succotash.

California Pizza Kitchen's Jambalaya

Another testament to CPK's diverse and creative offerings, one bite of this blackened chicken dynamo, and you'll recall the smooth jazz of the Big Easy. It doesn't stop at chicken though; andouille sausage and Tasso ham round out a hefty helping of proteins, kicked up a notch with a spicy jambalaya sauce.

BEST

T.G.I. Friday's Cajun Shrimp and Chicken Pasta

It's a favorite, it seems: take pasta and make it your own. T.G.I. Friday's upped the ante to creative permutations with this creamy Alfredo riff, mixed in with Cajun butter. Parmesan gives it an Italian touch, but the shrimp and chicken are no doubt partial to the Cajun palate. It's a perfect example of how to make pasta more than just pasta.

ENTRÉES

GOOD

T.G.I. Friday's Shrimp Key West

These babies are skewered and grilled—over an open flame. First dusted with Cajun seasonings and kissed with a ginger-lime dressing, they're just the right mix of sharp, hot, and prawniness. Freshly steamed broccoli and perhaps a side of rice adds to the satisfaction.

BETTER

Applebee's Cajun Lime Tilapia

It's got kick, it's got personality, and it recalls the glories of the Cajun South. A gentle fish, tilapia is seasoned with traditional Cajun spices and topped with lime juice. It's a happy plate-fellow for the likes of black beans, corn salsa, rice pilaf, and seasonal vegetables. This delicious treat is healthy, too!

BEST

Ruby Tuesday's New Orleans Seafood

This one is so popular, it's a standard on Ruby Tuesday's menu—Creole-touched tilapia (a Southern favorite) plus sautéed shrimp, all mixed in a rich Parmesan cream sauce. Signature from-scratch cheese biscuits treat the palate to a savory, northern alternative to the Big Easy's famed beignets.

ENTRÉES

GOOD

Hooters' Lots-a-Tots with Cajun Sauce

The next time you find yourself at Hooters, order a nice entrée-size portion of Tater Tots (Lots-a-Tots on the "Hooterstizers" apps menu, but who's counting?) and request a nice smothering of their Cajun sauce. True, this tangy, spicy drencher is usually reserved for their wings, but also true: the customer is always right.

BETTER

Mimi's Cafe's Cajun Chicken Alfredo

Speaking of substitutions, this one might amount to sacrilege. But it's a testament to the deliciousness of Mimi's Cajun Alfredo sauce that this pasta dish can be stripped of its Cajun-spiced chicken, roasted pork loin, and chicken andouille sausage and still taste awful darn good.

BEST

The Cheesecake Factory's Garlic Noodles

A stretch? Yes. But a yummy one at least: spaghetti, asparagus, shiitake mushrooms, oven-roasted tomatoes, and Parmesan cheese in a garlicky garlic sauce. Not exactly Cajun—perhaps not Cajun at all—but ask for a side of chile flakes, and you're on your way.

Justin Wilson
No mention of Cajun cuisine would be acceptable without a nod to our good man Justin Wilson, chef, humorist, author, and all-around promoter of all things Cajun. Wilson penned seven Cajun cookbooks and hosted several cooking shows on PBS. His tagline, a warm and heartfelt "I garontee!"

ENTRÉES

16

Italian Entrées

Perhaps no other cuisine category sings the chain restaurant mantra of "Fill 'em up and send 'em home with leftovers" quite like Italian. Big servings of beef, pikes of poultry, slabs of seafood, and of course, pounds and pounds of pasta all make for eminently satisfying experiences of stuffing yourself until you look—and sound—like Don Corleone.

While there are several chains specializing in Italian, it seems just about all of them have at least a couple of nods to "the boot." The reasons for this might be the breadth of Italian cuisine—which has changed radically over the centuries—and the fact that most dishes only require a handful of ingredients. Keep it simple, and keep it coming! *Mangia, mangia, mangia!*

GOOD

BETTER

Romano's Macaroni Grill's Veal Saltimbocca

Thin slices of veal pan-fried with rosemary ham and garlic and served over roman artichoke pasta—doesn't that just sound good? Take this also as a fine example of simplicity giving rise to something full-bodied, luscious, and delicious.

Buca di Beppo's Chianti-Braised Short Ribs

It's just about mathematically impossible to go wrong with beef short ribs, slow-braised and smothered in a tomato reduction made with Bucca di Beppo's famous house Chianti. The menu suggests trying these savory, tender wonders with a side of garlic mashed potatoes, but why not double down on a doubled heap of those to be sure every last bit of sauce is put to work?

BEST

Romano's Macaroni Grill's Florentine Steak and Frites

True, steak and frites are typically French fare, but there's no reason prime sirloin can't take a spot under some arugula pesto next to a mouthwatering pile of Parmesan fries and be called Italian. No matter what you call it, you can call yourself satisfied creating perfect bite after perfect bite of savory, buttery steak and salty, cheesy fries.

CHICKEN

GOOD

BETTER

Olive Garden's Chicken Scampi

Tender tenderloins—is there anything better? Sautéed with red bell peppers and tossed with roasted garlic and onions in a garlic cream sauce, this scampi rests on a bed of angel hair pasta. Don't forget the salad or soup and breadsticks that come with the deal.

Carino's Italian's Chicken Milano

The layers of goodness make this one a keeper: thick sautéed chicken breast, raised to the next level with plump mushrooms, ham, basil, melted provolone, and the creamiest of Alfredo sauces. As if you need more in all that flavor, it's paired with an al dente bed of fettuccine. *Delicioso!*

BEST

Buca di Beppo's Chicken Saltimbocca

Sometimes, the staples are hard to do right, but Buca hit a homerun with this entrée. The traditional flavors are present and accounted for—fresh sage, genuine prosciutto, capers, artichoke hearts, and the tangiest-smoothest lemon butter sauce you can imagine. The whole dish will warm your heart, and it might just make you swoon.

GOOD

Buca di Beppo's Ravioli with Meat Sauce

The meat sauce here is an utter classic, and for good reason: 100 percent premium ground beef abounds in every steaming ladleful. Several of those ladles bathe this generous portion of ravioli stuffed with four cheeses—mozzarella, provolone, Parmesan, and ricotta.

BETTER

Romano's Macaroni Grill's Mom's Ricotta Meatballs and Spaghetti

The question of who exactly Mom is lingers but is quickly overshadowed by the velvety richness of her meatballs. The richness comes from a blend of beef and veal made silky by the addition of ricotta cheese. Mom keeps you on your toes with crushed red chile.

BEST

Big Boy's Endless Pasta

Big Boy? Really? You ask. Well, yes. *Endless pasta!* You can eat as much as you want—it never stops. Meaty marinara (or zesty if you tire of the meat) is served over spaghetti or penne. Add to that a grilled garlic roll and a tossed or Caesar salad, and see if you can't expand yourself out of your least favorite pair of pants.

ENTRÉES

GOOD

The Cheesecake Factory's Pasta Da Vinci

Much like the creations of the man himself, the Pasta Da Vinci reconciles simplicity and ingenuity, arguing in favor of that old adage: "Simplicity is concise creativity." Chicken, onions, mushrooms, and a tantalizing Madeira sauce are all that's needed to make this bowl of pasta a work of art.

BETTER

California Pizza Kitchen's Pesto Cream Penne

Pesto is the foundation of Italian cooking. Okay, that might be a slight exaggeration, but every good Italian knows that a good pesto is beyond compare. It's no wonder CPK took up the challenge: creamy, basil-rich pesto tossed with sun-dried tomatoes, Parmesan, and tender morsels of chicken.

BEST

Carino's Italian's Grilled Chicken Bowtie Festival

Dressed to the nines—
bowties and all—this
fete of chicken and pasta
doesn't stoop to standards.
It begins, as all good dishes,
with crispy bacon, potent
garlic, feisty red onions,
and plump Roma tomatoes.
A sweet, juicy chicken
breast and a decadent
Asiago cream sauce fire this
specialito della casa beyond
the confines of a simple
bowl of pasta.

ENTRÉES

GOOD

BETTER

Buca di Beppo's Linguine Fruitti di Mare

The ocean's bounty—shrimp, baby clams, mussels, and calamari—bursts on a bed of imported linguine tossed with a fiery red clam sauce. The sea fruits have never had it so good. Neither have you.

Romano's Macaroni Grill's Lobster Ravioli

Lobster-stuffed ravioli in a piquant Chardonnay cream sauce. Simple and utterly crave-worthy. There's really nothing more to say other than "Get your own plate!"

BEST

Seaworthy Pasta
The National Pasta Association is a great place to find seafood pasta recipes for those looking for a little inspiration. Check out ilovepasta.org.

The Cheesecake Factory's Shrimp with Angel Hair

Just because The Cheesecake Factory's specialty is having no specialty (other than cheesecake, that is) perhaps it's a bit surprising that their seafood pasta takes the crown. Well, their big plump shrimp sautéed with herbs, lemon, and garlic, and thrown together with angel hair pasta, tomato, and fresh basil makes the grade, plain and simple.

ENTRÉES

GOOD

BETTER

Romano's Macaroni Grill's Mushroom Ravioli

Simply typing these words puts my salivary glands in overdrive: ravioli stuffed with porcini mushrooms and bathed in caramelized onions and a marsala cream sauce. Actually eating this dish, you run the risk of doing permanent damage to your ability to crave other foods. Proceed with caution.

Carino's Italian's Homemade Eggplant Parmigiana

This is a signature recipe, and it earns its homemade status because Carino's feels like home. The secret? No secret really, just plenty of TLC going into slabs of breaded, fried eggplant dressed with tomato sauce and served with spaghetti.

BEST

Buca di Beppo's Gnocchi al Telefono

For anyone out of the loop, gnocchi are potato dumplings cooked like pasta in salty water. They are delicious, filling, and fun as all get out to eat. Here, they're tossed with fresh mozzarella and dredged in a roasted garlic marinara with a kiss of cream. Good luck topping this experience.

ENTRÉES

GOOD

BETTER

The Cheesecake Factory's Shrimp Scampi

If you like garlic, there's no beating The Factory's scampi—imagine whole cloves of garlic, sautéed with a dry white wine, fresh basil, tomato, and of course, premium shrimp. This isn't the kind of shrimp you dish out at cocktail parties—this is for special occasions. Except you might want to eat it every day.

Romano's Macaroni Grill's Pan-Seared Branzino

Also known as European sea bass, branzino is a very versatile fish often used in Italian cooking, especially in coastal regions. At Macaroni Grill, it's pan-seared until cooked just through and served with vine-ripened tomatoes, peppery arugula, rich cannellini beans, and for a unique twist, fennel pollen—like sweet, intense fennel seed.

BEST

Tony Roma's Shrimp and Salmon Piccata

The chef happily recommends this sweet seafood combo, but the chef isn't the only one. There's a reason this is a menu staple—Norwegian salmon (some of the best in the world) is gently blanketed by a lemon-caper sauce, not to mention a mound of shrimp. There's no question this one's a keeper.

17

Mediterranean Entrées

In theory, Mediterranean offerings might be the healthiest of all chain cuisines. Olive oil, fresh fish, veggies, and pasta make for naturally heart-wise fare. But we're not just looking for clean arteries here; we're looking for indulgence, so here you'll find a thoughtful blend of breezy delights and regional richness.

Why the disparity? Well, the whole idea of a Mediterranean diet is a touch overblown anyway. They use lard and butter galore in northern Italy and that glass or two of red wine a day rife with antioxidants and blood-thinning power isn't so popular in the Muslim regions of the Med. So what follows is a celebration of diversity ... delicious diversity.

CHICKEN

GOOD

BETTER

Olive Garden's Mediterranean Grilled Chicken

Light and luscious, this herbaceous dish is zesty and personality-ridden without being overbearing. Too many cream sauces? This might tickle your palate: herb-marinated chicken breasts, a zesty lemon vinaigrette, cherry tomatoes, feta cheese, spinach, and olives. It's not just a feast for the mouth; it's a feast for the eyes.

Hard Rock Cafe's Lemon Caper Chicken

Boneless, unbelievably tender chicken is treated to some pampering at Hard Rock—grilled and gently garnished with Romano cheese, mushrooms, and fresh spinach. Served with a flavorful lemon-caper sauce and a heap of comforting ratatouille, this dish is both a delightful adventure and home away from home.

BEST

Ruby Tuesday's Chicken Fresco

The piquant, fiery, flavor-packed traditions of the Mediterranean aren't far from Ruby Tuesday's menu. This charactered dish renders weightier cousins almost obsolete: vine-ripened tomatoes at the peak of freshness, smooth but tangy lemon butter, and a splash of balsamic vinegar are all a tender breast of chicken needs for dressing. This dish speaks for itself.

LAMB

GOOD

Outback Steakhouse's New Zealand Lamb

Rich and tender with a slight gaminess (as all good lamb should be), this succulent treat is finished off with a velvety-smooth Cabernet sauce and is served with garlic mashed potatoes and fresh mixed veggies. The Outback knows what hits the spot.

BETTER

P.F. Chang's Wok-Seared Lamb

This lamb is prepared simply and lovingly, just like it would be on the coasts of the Mediterranean Sea. Marinated with scallions and sesame seeds; browned on the outside in a hot, hot wok; and served over cabbage with some cilantro—delicious is a deliciously familiar concept, no matter where you are on the globe!

BEST

P.F. Chang's Chengdu Spiced Lamb

P.F. Chang's not only has the largest selection of lamb dishes out there (as far as chain restaurants go), but their preparation is exquisite: cumin, mint, tomatoes, and yellow onions make a bold, delicious canvas for tender, marinated lamb. You could eat this every day of the week and not get tired of it.

SANDWICHES

GOOD

BETTER

Hard Rock Cafe's Blackened Fish of the Day Sandwich

Dill mayo, cucumber, crisp iceberg lettuce, fresh tomato, and sweet red onion salute to a blackened fillet with all the respect it deserves. And keep your mind—and palate—open for whatever's on the menu tomorrow because the fish of the day changes, well, daily.

T.G.I. Friday's The Ultimate Sicilian Chicken Sandwich

Yes, Sicily is technically a part of Italy, but its heritage extends through the Mediterranean— and its cuisine is highly influenced by surrounding flavors. Chicken breast, pepperoni, and ham combine in this meal on a loaf with Caesar vinaigrette for a trip through the wild breezes of the sea. Actual voyage not included.

BEST

Logan's Roadhouse's "My Big Fat Greek" Steak Sandwich

Steak is Logan's business, so why doubt their ability to Greek it up? This one is big, and it's got all the flavor punch you'd expect of a grilled sirloin, pickled onions, tzatziki, lettuce, tomato, and feta. Served up on ciabatta, it's a good idea to get some fries with that—sweet potato fries if you're feeling adventurous.

ENTRÉES

GOOD

BETTER

The Cheesecake Factory's Mahi Mahi Mediterranean

Say hello to crumb-crusted fresh mahimahi, tomatoes, artichokes, capers, fresh basil, and a balsamic vinaigrette. Sure, it's served over mashed potatoes, and yes, mahimahi is the Hawaiian name for this type of fish, found in tropical and subtropical waters the world over, but everything else is spot-on.

Romano's Macaroni Grill's Parmesan-Crusted Sole

Filet of sole, baby, it's your favorite dish. Even if it's not, it might soon be after digging in to this flaky beauty. For as drool-inducing as the fillet is, it's hard to pick the absolute best element of this offering, considering that lemon butter, capers, and sun-dried tomato orzo share the same plate.

BEST

Carino's Italian's Lemon-Pepper Mahi Mahi

Not to dwell on the mahimahi, but it's just so flipping good prepared in the light Mediterranean style, grilled and topped with artichokes, Roma tomatoes, and spinach and served in a lemon-butter-wine sauce. The accompanying angel hair pasta and fresh vegetables make this one filling and healthful.

ENTRÉES

VEGETARIAN

GOOD

Romano's Macaroni Grill's Wild Mushroom and Goat Cheese Flatbread

Flatbread so good that if it were big enough, you'd want to use it as a mattress each and every night. Alas, it's only big enough to sleep two hamsters, so better go ahead and just eat this horizontal wonder topped with wild 'shrooms, goat cheese, caramelized onions, truffle oil, and herbs.

BETTER

Buca di Beppo's Margherita Pizza

This pizza would make a great bed as well—so warm, so aromatic, blankets of cheese—but again, it's a touch too small for snoozing on. But who could sleep on fresh mozzarella, basil, and house pizza sauce anyway? Eat up!

BEST

The Cheesecake Factory's Evelyn's Favorite Pasta

Evelyn must get lots of hugs from strangers, because her favorite pasta is a definite favorite with vegetarians and meat-eaters alike. Why? It's easy: penne tossed with broccoli, oven-dried tomatoes, roasted eggplant, peppers, artichoke hearts, kalamata olives, garlic, and pine nuts. 'Nuff said.

ENTRÉES

18

Southwestern/ Mexican Entrées

Mexican cuisine might be the most widely represented on the menus of our nation's chains. No huge surprise, really, given Mexico is one of our nearest neighbors. And while the offerings that have trickled down (or, geographically, up) aren't usually true to their roots (burritos smothered in green chiles were conceived on our side of the border), those roots are still true. And that's basically what gave birth to Southwestern cuisine.

These offerings are wide and beloved and, like everything else so far, have been finely tuned for consistency and bursting flavor. Whether you're in the market for a salad, a glistening beef chimichanga, or a raft of nachos, our chains have you covered. They know what warms your heart by way of a full and content stomach, and ultimately want you to feel like *familia*.

GOOD

BETTER

Johnny Rockets' The Houston

Take that burger and make it burn, baby! How, baby? Like this: jalapeños and pepper Jack. Too hot, baby? Okay, how about some iceberg lettuce and fresh tomato to cool it down? Uh-oh. Look out, baby, here comes some housemade spicy sauce. Take cover, baby!

California Pizza Kitchen's Steak Tacos

You might not expect a fancy-pants West Coast pizza joint to know the first thing about tacos, but your expectations are California Pizza Kitchen's number-one target. Or so it would seem on the basis of these baddies. Steak, shredded cabbage, and ranchito sauce qualify these tacos as street food, making them some of the most authentic Mexican food anywhere in this book.

BEST

Red Robin's Burnin' Love Burger

Fried jalapeño rings make a repeat appearance on this zesty burger. Other players include a mouthwatering salsa, pepper Jack cheese, and cayenne seasoning right in the burger. And how about serving it on a jalapeño-cornmeal kaiser roll slathered with chipotle mayo for good measure? Yes, I thought so.

ENTRÉES

GOOD

BETTER

Red Robin's Ensenada Chicken Platter

Red Robin lays another golden egg with this serving of two juicy chicken breasts basted in Mexican seasonings and grilled until the Baja flavor spews from the seams. A side salad and a duo of dipping sauces round out the brilliance.

The Cheesecake Factory's Baja Chicken Tacos

What's life without Baja chicken tacos? A hollow thing as fragile as an empty hard taco shell. True, these come on soft corn tortillas, but none of that is of any concern once the flavors of spicy chicken, cheese, avocado, tomato, onions, and cilantro blast your palate.

BEST

Chili's Crispy Chicken Tacos

Usually, tacos enjoy the filling of grilled morsels of chicken goodness, but what if someone were to batter and fry them first? Genius! Thank you, Chili's, for taking us where we've never gone before—complete with applewood-smoked bacon, tomatoes, cheese, lettuce, honey-chipotle drizzle, and ranch dressing. Finger-lickin' good.

Ancient Tacos

According to Sophie Averin, author of *History of Tortillas and Tacos*, the taco predates the European invasion of South America, with anthropologists citing evidence that the people living in the lake region of the Valley of Mexico ate tacos filled with small fish.

ENTRÉES

FAJITAS

GOOD

BETTER

T.G.I. Friday's Sizzling Chicken and Cheese

Inspired by the traditional fajita platter, this ooey-gooey dish twists tradition a bit by swapping tortillas for mashed potatoes and covering the whole skillet with cheese—Mexican cheese. The heart of the dish alone is worth a foray into something slightly new: two plump chicken breasts on a bed of onions and peppers. T.G.I.F., indeed.

Chili's Fajita Trio

Three is better than one, right? Of course it is. Dig it: a sizzling platter of grilled steak, tender chicken, and garlic-and-lime shrimp all dished up on a bed of caramelized bell peppers and onions. This might be your best bet if you can't decide what kind of fajita to get—or if you're just ravenously hungry.

BEST

Hard Rock Cafe's Famous Fajitas

Why is it famous? Because (1) it's from Hard Rock Cafe, and (2) it's got a mouthwatering list of possibilities: chicken, beef, shrimp, chicken and beef, chicken and shrimp, beef and shrimp, beef and beef—well, you get the idea. It's hard to beat that kind of meat—served up with pico de gallo, shredded Jack and cheddar cheeses, guac, sour cream, lettuce, and hot flour tortillas.

QUESADILLAS

GOOD

BETTER

Mimi's Cafe's BBQ Pork Quesadilla

Want a shareable plate of gooey goodness? Of course you do, which is why you want Mimi's quesadilla—spread with barbecued pulled pork, Jack cheese, and green onions. A side of tangy coleslaw keeps your mouth watering for another order.

The Cheesecake Factory's Quesadilla

Sticking to the basics is never bad form. Proof: grilled flour tortillas filled with melty cheese, green onions, and chiles. Garnish? Oh, alright: guacamole, salsa, and sour cream.

BEST

Big Boy's Chicken Quesadilla

Picture this: all-white chicken meat with melted pepper Jack and cheddar cheeses, grilled green pepper, and red onion with some salsa and sour cream on the side. Can you picture it? Okay. Now order it!

ENTRÉES

GOOD

BETTER

T.G.I. Friday's Chipotle Yucatan Chicken Salad

A delightful diorama of seasoned, blackened chicken, pulled and put to good use in a salad of mixed greens and romaine, topped with avocado, tomato, cheeses, and tostada chips. Over top, an avocado vinaigrette. Best eaten on the Yucatan or anywhere else.

The Cheesecake Factory's Grilled Chicken Tostada Salad

Let me break it down for you: crispy corn tortillas piled with grilled marinated chicken breast, black beans, mixed greens, fresh corn, green onions, and cilantro tossed in a house vinaigrette and dolloped with avocado cream, salsa, and sour cream. Here's to getting delightfully lost in the ingredients list alone.

BEST

Red Robin's Southwest Grilled Chicken Salad

Certainly not your daddy's Southwest chicken salad, this iconoclast takes ancho-grilled chicken, avocado slices, and fried jalapeño coins and sets them alight on a dance floor of crisp greens tossed in salsa-ranch dressing. Diced peppers and onions, chipotle black beans, cheddar and pepper Jack cheeses, and crunchy tortilla strips punctuate the presentation.

ENTRÉES

GOOD

BETTER

Tony Roma's Blackened Salmon with Kickin' Sauce

Yes, you have the option to pick your seasoning and topping, but really, there's only one "best" you should consider: blackened with Kickin' Sauce. It's got heft, it's got flavor, it's got, well, it's just really good. Keep it simple with rice and veggies, and you'll have yourself to thank for a healthy meal that leaves you satiated.

Applebee's Spicy Pineapple Glazed Shrimp and Spinach

Sweet? Now that's an idea. Pineapple-glazed shrimp, skewered and grilled atop white rice. Black bean and corn salsa? Why not. And then there's the kicker: tender spinach salad. It's not quite what you expect from the Southwest, and yet, by golly, it's good!

BEST

Logan's Roadhouse's Santa Fe Tilapia

Tilapia, that gentle and delicate fish, has found a home at Logan's. TLC gives it a touch of spice—not too much, mind you—and lays it down with a roasted corn and black bean salsa for company. In case you fear the lack of zest, don't. A cilantro-chipotle sauce offers everything you need in that department.

VEGETARIAN

GOOD

BETTER

Hard Rock Cafe's Hard Rock Nachos

Appetizer you say? Poppycock. This is billed as big enough to share, and in chain lingo, that's just code for "entrée." And a meal this is, what with tortilla chips lost under mounds of Jack and cheddar cheeses and seasoned pinto beans. A bevy of accoutrements—sour cream, chopped green onions, pico de gallo, jalapeños, and Hard Rock Grilled Salsa—make this fun eating, indeed.

Chili's Guiltless Grill Santa Fe Wrap

You know, it comes with chicken, but who needs that? Crispy tortilla strips provide the crunch, cheddar cheese gives it some creaminess, avocado rounds it out, and tomatoes add a touch of color. Oh, let's not forget about the spicy kick of the ancho-chile ranch. Why, with all that in your mouth, there's no room for meat!

BEST

California Pizza Kitchen's Tostada Pizza

Once again, Wolfgang Puck's crown jewel shows you a thing or two about tinkering with tradition. Here, black beans and cheddar and Jack cheeses get some dough for a good hearth-baking before being topped with chilled lettuce, scallions, tortilla strips, and homemade herb ranch dressing. The roasted tomato salsa on the side completes this delicious dish.

ENTRÉES

19

Steak Entrées

In the realm of chain eating, steaks are generally thought of as the domain of high-priced big boys like Morton's, Sullivan's, Del Frisco's, and Ruth's Chris, but you needn't drop tons of cash to get tons of quality and flavor where red meat is concerned.

Truth is, plenty of less-expensive chain restaurants take just as much pride in the selection and preparation of their steaks. You can saddle up to any of the selections in this chapter with confidence and steak knife in hand, knowing your meaty cravings are destined to be satisfied.

FILETS

GOOD

BETTER

Texas Roadhouse's Dallas Filet

You'd expect Texans to know a thing or two about steak, and their namesake roadhouse proves its mettle with this succulent filet. Available in 6- and 8-ounce cuts, this lean puck of meaty perfection can be smothered with the Roadhouse's special mix of accoutrements: sautéed mushrooms, sautéed onions, and choice of brown gravy or Jack cheese.

LongHorn Steakhouse's Flo's Filet

You'll likely want to find Flo and give her an extended hug after working your way through this tender, delicious cut. It's juicy, too. This is a LongHorn house specialty, and the kitchen does it right every time. Choice of side, salad, and forever freshly baked Honey Wheat bread seals the juicy, tender, delicious, juicy (yes, *that* juicy) deal.

BEST

**Outback Steakhouse's
The Melbourne**

Okay, so this is actually
a giant porterhouse, but
it's really a buttery strip
and a buttery, buttery
filet tenderloin in one
sumptuous cut. Maybe
that's not the purest way to
sweep this category, but it
sure is the most delicious
way to take the crown.
Perfectly seasoned and
grilled to perfection, this
one hits on every meaty
cylinder.

ENTRÉES

RIB EYES

GOOD

BETTER

Applebee's 12-Ounce Rib-Eye

This tender and flavorful cut of USDA Select rib eye is nicely marbled and just as nicely cooked to order. A helping of seasonal vegetables and garlic mashed potatoes or a baked potato seal the heat-seared deal.

Outback Steakhouse's Ribeye

There's not a lot to say about the rib eye steak. The meat is the meat, the fat is the flavor, and the heat brings the two into juicy delicious congress. Outback knows this well, and their rib eye is a testament to this primal and simply refined delicacy.

BEST

Texas Roadhouse's Bone-In Ribeye

Once again, simple is as simple does right with a rib eye. This one happens to be the biggest cut on the Roadhouse menu—at 20 juicy ounces—and could probably feed two if it weren't so hard for just one person to stop eating.

International Rib Eyes

In New Zealand, a rib eye is known as a Scotch filet or a "Scotchie." Despite being in another hemisphere, the cooking instructions remain the same: season lightly and sear over (or down under) high heat, leaving some pink.

ENTRÉES

GOOD

BETTER

The Cheesecake Factory's Chargrilled Coulotte Steak

This is such a good idea, it ought to be copied everywhere. This chargrilled prime sirloin is buttered and served with fries and onion rings. You can almost picture that perfect bite: a triangle of succulent steak perched on the fork and surrounded by an onion ring and crisscrossed by two fries.

LongHorn Steakhouse's Renegade Top Sirloin

This lovely USDA Choice sirloin is available in three sizes to suit your appetite: 6, 8, and 12 ounces. Order with a Parmesan or bleu cheese crust for an extra decadent treat. For crazy decadence, get a lobster tail on the side and tell them it's your birthday.

BEST

Applebee's 7-Ounce House Sirloin

A manageable and delicious 7-ounce cut drenched in seasoned butter and served with loaded mashed potatoes and steamed broccoli, this is a meal of refinement, class, and utter deliciousness. Lighter-minded patrons can help themselves to an extra heap of vegetables, but it's not quite the same without the mashed potatoes.

ENTRÉES

STRIPS

GOOD

BETTER

Outback Steakhouse's New York Strip

The muscle behind this cut isn't used for much, so it's extra tender. Most New York strips, this one included, have ample fat content, giving the cut so much flavor it's usually a shame to cover up what's naturally there with a sauce or a crust.

Texas Roadhouse's New York Strip

Any Texan will tell you that Texas ain't New York, but that doesn't mean the Texas Roadhouse isn't a master of this coveted cut of short loin. This is a hand-cut New York strip—juicy and cooked to order—flanked by two of Texas Roadhouse's legendary from-scratch sides like seasoned rice or a baked sweet potato.

BEST

Logan's Roadhouse's NY Strip Steak

Not only does it weigh in at an impressive 11 ounces, but this juicy, tender strip has all the flavorings of a steak to remember. Hand-cut from Midwestern Black Angus beef (only the best at Logan's), it's flame-grilled over mesquite wood to lock in the juices and give it a little bit of subtle flavor. Pair it with fries, veggies, a beer, or onion rings.

ENTRÉES

Desserts

20

Baked Treats

Baked goods are central to our diet—and, let's face it, our appetites. But there's more to these sweet treats than sugar and dough. There are memories of childhood, intermingled with grandparents and parents. We recall Christmases past, holidays with family, and celebrations every time we bite into a cookie, a brownie, or a piece of decadent chocolate cake.

Which is why, despite medical admonitions, we would never give up these quintessential comfort foods. There's more to life than diet, after all, and each of the exceptional baked goods in this chapter reminds us of that very fact. Perhaps it even inspires us to carry on a tradition, to pass down a recipe, to begin our own family rituals. There's nothing quite like a freshly baked chocolate-chip cookie, after all—particularly when it conjures so many happy memories.

BROWNIES

GOOD

Chili's Brownie Sundae

Nothing sweetens a sweet tooth quite like a brownie—the decadence of chocolate coupled with the richness of butter and the right amount of sugar. And in this case, a heap of vanilla ice cream is included, just in case you need something to cut the chocolate. Oh, and it's also drizzled with hot fudge, just as an added precaution.

BETTER

Hard Rock Cafe's Hot Fudge Brownie

It's hot. It's fudgy. And it's … gone? Yep, it's that delicious—Ben & Jerry's 'nilla ice cream and hot fudge top a freshly baked brownie with walnuts. Not that such a delight needs embellishments, but here they are anyway: chocolate sprinkles, fresh whipped cream, and a cherry on top.

BEST

Sunday Sundae?
Like so many classics, the sundae has a disputed birthplace. Was it created by a minister in Ithaca at the turn of the nineteenth century, or perhaps by Edward C. Berners at his soda fountain shop in 1881? And was it really created on a Sunday?

Logan's Roadhouse's Big and Chewy Hot Fudge Brownie

There's nothing special about this brownie, you say? Nonsense. It needs no pomp simply because its simplicity is all it needs. Get that? It's deep chocolate in a portion to rival your entrée, capped by the viscous goodness of hot fudge. Sometimes, chocolate speaks well on its own.

DESSERTS

GOOD

BETTER

Denny's Hershey's Chocolate Cake

Imagine it: layers of Hershey's chocolatey goodness, cake and crunch, combined with whipped cream, dished up with curls of chocolate. Okay, now you can stop imagining it and actually order it—before the meal, of course.

California Pizza Kitchen's Red Velvet Cake

Don't ever shun tradition—there's a reason the classics have been around for so long. Case in point: CPK's Red Velvet Cake of Deliciousness. Moist layers, vanilla bean cream cheese, and white chocolate curls are all it takes to get your mouth watering. But think before you order. Don't you want to have that with some Häagen-Dazs ice cream?

BEST

The Cheesecake Factory's Chocolate Tower Truffle Cake

The Factory's desserts are no doubt legendary—both in flavor and in size. This one takes the cake, so to speak, with more chocolate than you know what to do with. It's recommended that you just eat it. Layer upon layer of fudgy cake alternates with chocolate truffle cream and chocolate mousse. Sharing is allowed, but not expected.

> **Cake History**
> The word *cake* descends from the Viking word *kaka,* which roughly means "sweet confection." The oldest evidence of baking, however, dates to ancient Egypt, where they would often make breadlike confections sweetened with honey.

DESSERTS

GOOD

Bob Evans' Coconut Cream Pie

Coconuty, creamy, and whipped goodness. Now, before you drool on anything or anyone, compose yourself long enough to order this luscious, coconut-filled, sweet cream-topped, toasted coconut-garnished delectable dessert extravaganza.

BETTER

Village Inn's Cherry Pie

Some say the crust makes the pie. Others say the filling makes the pie. Others just eat it and never wonder why. You won't have time to ponder much once a slice of this sweet cherry pie comes your way—between two layers of signature flaky crust that would make Mom jealous. Never fear; you can bring her home a slice, too.

BEST

Award-Winning Pie
Valerie Enters of Los Angeles has been winning pie contests since 2006, when her cherry pie took top honors at the National Pie Competition.

Perkins' Peanut Butter Silk Pie

If chocolate cures all that ails you, then chocolate and peanut butter pie puts you on cloud nine. There are so many layers to this pie it's tongue boggling: hard chocolate ganache, Reese's peanut butter silk, whipped cream, and mini Reese's cups. If you were thinking about ordering a hot fudge chaser, think again. This pie is richer than the Sultan of Brunei.

DESSERTS

21
Even More Desserts

Wherever our cultural palate lies, or whatever path it currently explores, there's never a shortage of imagination when it comes to creating desserts. In fact, we enjoy desserts so much we've begun adding them to dinner—in fine-dining restaurants no less!

While the staples will always be staples (how could we ever denounce pie or disown chocolate cake?), there are always forays into the new. From one-time traditional ice cream sundaes come all flavors and concoctions, all layers and combinations. We've even taken hold of international tastes, adopting dishes like tiramisu and running with the idea. Stretching from traditional scoops of ice cream to banal crisps, there are now hundreds of dishes we call our own that embrace both a measure of comfort and an air of creativity. How could we possibly not give a nod to those which now unwaveringly hold our attention?

GOOD

Mimi's Cafe's Fresh Apple Cinnamon Crisp

It's down-home Sundays with Grandma in a dessert! Plump, fresh apples are tossed with sugar and baked under the buttery crunch of golden streusel and topped with a scoop of vanilla ice cream. If you're not satisfied with trying just one dessert, keep in mind you can get the Ensemble and indulge, indulge, indulge.

BETTER

Cracker Barrel's Baked Apple Dumplin'

What a crock of … apples? Oh, indeed—and the best part is, this crisp has a crust underneath! Filled with cinnamony delicious apples and topped with pecan streusel, you'll be talking about the Dumplin' 'til the cows come home! This is the definition of American comfort food, and don't you forget it.

BEST

Don't Knock Crisps
Some call a crisp the lazy man's pie. But then, those are the same people who buy premade piecrusts at the grocery store.

Red Robin's Apple Bites

Somehow, it's reminiscent of the fall in New England and childhood at Christmastime, while also being totally innovative. Juicy pieces of Fuji, Gala, and Granny Smith apples are simmered in a sweet filling and then magically transformed into deep-fried bites. Welcome to your new happy place.

DESSERTS

GOOD

BETTER

Bennigan's S'mores Sundae

Childhood comes alive, and the memory of roasting marshmallows floods back with this all-American treat. A s'mores brownie (read: deliciousness) is topped by a skewer of toasted marshmallows and drizzled with epic chocolate sauce. And there's a scoop of vanilla ice cream in there somewhere, too.

Johnny Rockets' Single Scoop

Remember the diners of the 1960s? Johnny Rockets has the feel down, and the ice cream. Enjoy a single scoop of premium vanilla and reminisce about the good old days. If you're especially nostalgic, consider upgrading to a Super Sundae and get all the fixins.

BEST

All Aboard!

In 1999, Royal Caribbean International cruises featured Johnny Rockets onboard one of its ships, making it the first such mobile restaurant in the history of chain restaurants.

T.G.I. Friday's Oreo Madness

A new confectionery treat on the menu, Oreo Madness makes you feel like you're getting away with something you shouldn't. Cookies and cream ice cream is tucked between two layers of Oreo cookie and drizzled with caramel and fudge. Oreo cookie dipping just took on a whole new meaning.

DESSERTS

TIRAMISU

GOOD

BETTER

Romano's Macaroni Grill's Tiramisu

It's a classic Italian dessert … and an American appropriation! Macaroni Grill certainly does the age-old dessert justice, using fresh mascarpone cheese, ladyfingers, espresso, coffee, and a spirited touch—rum. It starts out rich and creamy and bites back with the alcohol, all ending smoothly in chocolaty delight.

Olive Garden's Tiramisu

Beginning first with a layer of espresso-soaked ladyfingers, the dish rises with creamy mascarpone cheese and a top hat of finely grated cocoa powder. Be sure to order a strong cup of coffee to go with this temptation—the two play very well together.

BEST

Tiramisu Spirits

Possible liqueurs to use when making a tiramisu include Madeira, cognac, rum, coffee liqueur, brandy, and port. Use one or all as desired.

Carino's Italian's Homemade Tiramisu

Carino's believes in layering flavors—and their tiramisu, which is why you'll find three layers of espresso-soaked ladyfingers alternating with a rich, sweet Italian custard. The libation of choice in this creation, however, is not just rum, but rum *and* coffee liqueur. Eat slowly, and savor the sweetness.

Special Offerings and Features

22

Special Offerings

As mentioned at the beginning of this odyssey, chain restaurants get a bad rap for their careful homogenous nature. Generally speaking, everything is attended to just so, so your Applebee's/Macaroni Grill/Red Robin/Waffle House experience in one zip code feels über-familiar in another. It's a sweat-and-blood tango really, as restaurants are, by their very nature, places that invite chaos.

Amidst all that chaos (and all the other chaos in the world), chain restaurants stand sturdy and at the watch. And for as much as independent restaurants vary from one another, chain restaurants have their own ways of standing out as well. Sometimes it's through charitable donations of time, money, and product, sometimes it's with a stellar wine list, and other times it's with health-conscious menu additions. In this chapter, I share a variety of standout items and actions to pique your interest and whet your appetite for more.

GOOD

The Cheesecake Factory's Smoked Salmon Platter

Traditional breakfast might mean two eggs, sausage, and toast, but there's a new game in town: lox. The Factory's tapped into the wealth of Scandinavia with this treat, boasting fresh smoked salmon, cream cheese, tomato, red onion, and a delicious bagel. Eat it all separately or make a little open-faced breakfast sandwich; either way, you may never go back to eggs again.

BETTER

Ruby Tuesday's Sunrise Quesadilla

A quesadilla before noon? Surely not! Ah, surely so. And this one's a keeper: try some Swiss cheese, avocado, and bacon (and why not add cheddar for good measure) to hit the day running. If you're brave, you might also ask for a fried egg on top, although that's just unheard of. Or is it?

BEST

Big Boy's Sunrise Slim Jim

You've definitely heard of breakfast sandwiches, but this might take your breath away: ham, Swiss cheese, and egg layered with special Big Boy sauce on a grilled roll, dished up with a side of hash browns. This one might be good enough to order for lunch, too—or heck, for a midday snack. Just don't forget to ask for a little extra special sauce.

Big Boy Breakfasts

Breakfast is not only the most important meal of the day; it's the only meal worth repeating morning, noon, and night. Is it any wonder Big Boy is loved so?

GOOD

BETTER

Outback Steakhouse's Filet Focaccia Sandwich

This rich filet sandwich has all the makings of a satisfying meal, sacrificing nothing for a diet—including a delicious filet, melty provolone cheese, and garlic-herb aïoli on toasted bread. Served *au jus*, there's not much more you can ask for. As is, it clocks in at about 850 calories, but if you want to cut back even more, consider skipping the cheese.

T.G.I. Friday's Petite Sirloin

You may be watching what you eat, but you don't have to watch it too closely. Any restaurant that can offer sirloin for dieters is to be sought after, no doubt, and T.G.I. Friday's has made it happen: a juicy, tender, 6-ounce fillet, fire-grilled and served with ginger-lime slaw and fresh broccoli. It's a mountain of flavor for a paltry 750 calories. Take that to the diet bank and cash it.

BEST

Chili's Grilled Salmon with Garlic and Herbs

No guilt, no fuss, but all the flavor. Chili's has done right by health-conscious diners with this option: fresh, flaky salmon grilled with a special collection of herbs and dished up with rice pilaf and steamed broccoli. It may not sound like much, but you'll be pleasantly surprised when you spend 580 calories on an astoundingly satisfying meal. Cheers to that!

Red Meat: Yes or No? Why is red meat good for you, anyway? Word has it, red meat is high in zinc, a supporter of healthy immunity, not to mention iron (widely used the body over) and complete proteins. The downside: red meat is heavy in saturated fats and cholesterol.

GLUTEN-FREE OPTIONS

GOOD

BETTER

The Cheesecake Factory

Although it doesn't boast a ton of gluten-free options (surprising, given the vast number of menu items), The Factory does have a respectable number of tasty salads and entrées for celiacs, including the Grilled Salmon and Mahi Mahi. Add on a side of green beans or spinach, and you'll find it to be quite a satisfactory meal. Sadly, The Cheesecake Factory does not offer any gluten-free cheesecakes.

Applebee's

Hats off to 'bee's, where they go all-out to provide dining options for those with all types of allergies—including wheat. From appetizers to desserts (one of the hardest courses to offer something gluten-free), they produce excellent dishes. Care for Smothered Grilled Chicken perhaps, coupled with Mexi Rice and a Hot Fudge Sundae chaser? Dig in.

BEST

Outback Steakhouse

These days, it's almost a given that restaurants would have a list of vegetarian options—even if they're a steakhouse. But gluten-free? Rest assured that won't be a problem at Outback. They have a whole menu dedicated to celiac-intolerant diners, who can happily indulge in everything from succulent ribs to tenderloin and tuna without worrying about what will and won't work for them.

GOOD

BETTER

Red Robin's Garden Burger

Garden burgers are hit or miss at best—and you don't want to miss. Don't be wary of this monumental burger, though; it's got everything a veggie-lover could ask for. Start with a whole-grain bun, and top it with a Gardenburger (you know the name), tomatoes, lettuce, pickles, and Country Dijon Sauce. Like all Red Robin creations, this one is a mouthful—and comes with the traditional bottomless basket of fries.

California Pizza Kitchen's Vegetarian Pizza with Japanese Eggplant

There's something slightly exotic about this dish, but at the same time, it brings home the comfort of housemade pizza. And with the meatiness of the eggplant, you'll never know it lacks meat (if that's something you were worried about anyway). Add goat cheese for extra creaminess, and ask for a honey wheat crust if you want the full treatment.

BEST

Buca di Beppo's Pastas

Buca wins the crown in this category, not because of only one dish—although the Baked Ravioli will take your breath away—but because there are so many—and so many good ones—to choose from! Cheese Manicotti, Fettuccine Alfredo, Baked Ziti—you name it. Each one is as good as the next, rich and clearly filled with Italian TLC.

GOOD

BETTER

The Cheesecake Factory

A perfect match to the impressive breadth of the lunch and dinner menus at The Cheesecake Factory is their spectacular wine list. Plenty of reds, whites, and sparklers from all over the globe are represented here, including a signature Chardonnay and Cabernet Sauvignon, both produced exclusively for The Factory by Robert Mondavi.

Olive Garden

Be warned, only the breadsticks and salad are bottomless here, not the house wines. But there are three to savor: a red, a blush, and a white, perfect for mixing and matching to Olive Garden's imitable menu of Italian goodies. This holy trinity is joined by a lovely list of fellow russos, rosatos, and biancos, as well as some bubbly spumante to get the party started.

BEST

Romano's Macaroni Grill

You can't do Italian properly without a selection of fine wines, and it should come as no surprise that Macaroni Grill has a real banger. A house chardonnay and Chianti are joined by a thoughtful list of global grape juice, including a La Marca DOC Prosecco from Italy, perfect for celebrations.

GOOD

BETTER

Applebee's Skinny Bee Margarita

Poured with Hornitos Tequila and around 100 calories—and that's pretty cool when you realize you burn 3 calories just by lifting your glass to take a sip. Applebee's notes that it's perfect for drinking while sharing a laugh with friends and reminds you that laughing burns an additional 1.3 calories per minute. So drink this with your funniest friends!

Ruby Tuesday's Açaí Mojito

Craving a healthy mojito? Step right up to one bursting with antioxidants. VeeV Açaí Spirit (billed as the world's first Açaí spirit), joins freshly muddled mint, fresh-squeezed lime juice, agave nectar, and pomegranate in this bold and beautiful creation. We've heard that seven of these a day keeps the doctor away, but we can't recommend that.

BEST

Romano's Macaroni Grill's Margarita Prima

Rarely does one find tequila in an Italian restaurant. In this case, however, Macaroni Grill has ventured beyond the norm to bring you a new take on the classic margarita. Milagro Silver Tequila is the foundation, upon which is built Tuaca (an Italian vanilla-citrus liqueur), agave nectar, and lemon juice. Sip and savor; this will change the way you see a margarita.

The Tuaca

Once upon a time, Tuaca earned its place in the world of libations as a favorite of Lorenzo de Medici in the courts of Florence. It fell away from favor after the reign of the Medicis but was rediscovered in 1938 and became a popular drink for servicemen during World War II. These days, it's taken on a character of its own, being mixed or enjoyed straight the world over for its unique combination of vanilla and citrus flavors.

23

Special Features

These days, diners demand seamless experiences when they're out for a meal, and that means making sure the restaurants where they eat can accommodate their needs and preferences—everything from an experiential bent to a menu with a wide variety of dishes for the choosing. These are some of the restaurants we thought offered special features for dining, along with what makes them unique.

GOOD

BETTER

Applebee's

A salute to veterans from the whole team—and many a guest—at Applebee's, the Honor a Veteran program is one way to share your thanks for a vet's service to his or her country. More than 700,000 folks have offered their support, gratitude, and pictures memorializing the sacrifice servicemen and -women have given to the U.S. of A. Visit applebees.com to add your thanks.

Ruby Tuesday

Hats off to Ruby Tuesday, where giving back is just part of doing good business. The basics are covered here, with funds being donated regularly to Second Harvest Food Bank of Tennessee and Blount County Educational Foundation. Ruby Tuesday also has developed a Relief Fund that supports Ruby team members afflicted by natural and manmade disasters.

BEST

Hard Rock Cafe

"Love All, serve All" is what Hard Rock is all about, which translates to doing in local and global communities. Their partnerships and philanthropic participation are mind-boggling, with charitable activities benefiting Amnesty International, Breast Cancer Research Foundation, Children's Miracle Network, WHY Hunger, and more than a dozen other organizations.

Doing Good

Charitable giving by restaurants is no new thing. Many a chain and local eatery are giving back to their communities. Subway gave $10,000 to weather victims in Alabama in 2011, while Smashburger became a supporter of Camp CARE, an organization dedicated to helping families—especially kids—with cancer. In a different way, many chains are reaching out to the needy in communities by offering jobs. Pizza Fusion in Denver, for example, hired several new employees from the local homeless community, providing them with much needed job experience and training.

GOOD

T.G.I. Friday's

An environment so bustling that screaming kids barely make a dent—that's one allure here. The kid's menu is another. And Friday's offers staples like mac 'n' cheese and hot dogs joined by more fun stuff like chicken skewers and a whole list of slushies and smoothies. Best of all, the beloved Cup of Dirt: chocolate pudding, crumbled Oreos, and a gummy worm.

BETTER

Red Lobster

Dining out should be all about fun—and not worrying what the kids are getting into. Never fear, Red Lobster has you covered with a kids' menu that introduces tikes to the likes of Popcorn Shrimp and Broiled Fish. But there's also a slew of common favorites, including Mac and Cheese and Chicken Fingers. And for dessert? A Surf's Up Sundae!

BEST

Shoney's

Shoney's bills itself as a family-friendly restaurant, and they live up to their word. This is a place you can come with the whole family any time of day. Rest assured that the kids' menu gives everyone what they want—happy parents, happy kids. Spaghetti, Grilled Cheese, and Pizza dot the menu, as well as an impressive buffet, should you have a little one with the appetite of a big one.

Cuisine Kid
At the tender age of 7, Chef Justin Miller began his professional cooking career. That was long after moving past the burger and pizza stage; in fact, his culinary repertoire was so sophisticated, he published his own cookbook, featuring the likes of French toast and pork chops (although not in the same dish).

ENVIRONMENTALLY FRIENDLY

GOOD

BETTER

Hard Rock Cafe

Hard Rock's environmental work spreads far and wide, from partnering with The Association of Zoos and Aquariums to sell pins to raise money for endangered species; to Earth Hour celebrations in Jakara, Bali, and Bangkok, where diners ate by candlelight and enjoyed acoustic concerts on March 26, 2011; to supporting Neil Young's LincVolt Project, to create "clean automobile propulsion technology."

Waffle House's Project Green House

Working to build a better environment, one waffle at a time, the Waffle House has undertaken Project Green House—a sustainability effort that includes recycling, conservation, and product savings. In 2010, Waffle House recycled more than 756 tons of cardboard and paper and 94.5 tons each aluminum and plastic. That equates to a lot of energy, which means a lot more Earth-friendly waffles.

BEST

Ruby Tuesday

Ruby Tuesday takes "going green" to the next level, challenging its suppliers to be kind to the environment in their product sourcing and distributing. In addition, at a hospitality facility dubbed the RT Lodge, employees get regular education on how the brand is implementing green strategies and how to ensure they're maintained at every restaurant.

GOOD

BETTER

Buca di Beppo

The fact that several Buca di Beppo locations have a lazy Susan with a bust of the pope in the middle of the big round table for large groups counts as an experience all on its own. Add to that experience the aura of a madcap Italian carnival—walls adorned with scads of framed, vintage photos and plenty of glowing lightbulbs—and you've got yourself a cozy and incredibly vibrant dining experience.

Hard Rock Cafe

One of the best ways to experience rock 'n' roll is at Hard Rock Cafe, where you're surrounded by unique memorabilia. And no two cafes are alike. Items at the Denver location, for example, include a toboggan used by The Beatles in the film *Help!*, the frilly cat suit Steven Tyler wore in Aerosmith's "Ragdoll" video, and a typewriter Hunter S. Thompson typed on … and then shot with a gun.

BEST

Waffle House

Why Waffle House, you ask? Well, while the Hard Rock Cafe pleases patrons with preselected rock and roll hits, Waffle House puts you behind the turntables. Well, sort of. Every Waffle House has a jukebox, and some even have table-side units that play old 45s. Bonus: Waffle House restaurants are open 24 hours a day, so you can literally rock around the clock.

GOOD

BETTER

Chili's

Chili's is one of America's favorite restaurant sons. Part of the appeal is absolutely the variety of dishes offered. Hungry for meat? Ribs, steaks, and chicken dishes abound. Have a hankering for Tex-Mex? Take your pick of a number of quesadillas or fajita platters. And the variety doesn't stop with the food; beers, cocktails, and wines are remarkably plentiful for a restaurant with no fine-dining pretension.

California Pizza Kitchen

Sure, "pizza" is in the name, but it doesn't stop there. Take your pick of salads, appetizers, sandwiches, entrées, and desserts enough to meet any picky eater's requirements. And if you came for the pizza, you'll be pleasantly surprised. More than two dozen varieties with the option to change toppings makes CPK a popular haunt for anyone who digs the pie.

BEST

The Cheesecake Factory

If you haven't seen the giant menu here, odds are you've at least heard about it. There's literally something for every taste, be it the evergreen New Selections section, the small plates huddle, the apps attack, a pizza or a "Glamburger," pasta, seafood, steaks, combo meals, or salads. Multiple world cuisines are present in each category, making deciding on something work enough to build a big appetite.

SPECIAL OFFERINGS & FEATURES